8 KEYS TO SELF LEADERSHIP

FROM AWARENESS TO ACTION

DARIO NARDI

UNITE
BUSINESS PRESS
A DIVISION OF TELOS PUBLICATIONS

Published By:
Unite Business Press, A Division of Telos Publications
P.O. Box 4457, Huntington Beach, California 92605-4457
Toll Free 1-866-416-8973 / Phone 1-714-965-7696 / Fax 1-714-965-7697
http://www.telospublications.com

Understanding Yourself and Others and *The Communication Zone* are registered trademarks of Unite Media Group, Inc., Fountain Valley, California. *Myers-Briggs Type Indicator*, *MBTI*, and *Myers-Briggs* are trademarks or registered trademarks of the Myers-Briggs Type Indicator Trust in the United States and other countries. *The Platinum Rule* is a registered trademark of Anthony J. Allessandra, Henderson, Nevada.

PRINTED IN THE UNITED STATES OF AMERICA

Cover Design: Judah Ben'Joshua
Layout Design/Illustrations: Visibility Designs
Chapter Cartoon Illustrations: Joe Kohl ((c) Unite Media Group, Inc.)

Library of Congress Cataloging-in-Publication Data

Acknowledgements

For this book I owe a great debt to many thinkers and colleagues. In addition to the writings of Carl Jung, Isabel Myers, and Walter Lowen, I thank foremost Linda V. Berens for ten years of thoughtful and insightful dialog about the cognitive processes and related models. I also thank colleagues Steve Myers, Lenore Thompson, John Beebe, Roger Pearman, Gary Hartzler, and Danielle Poirier. Without their experience and their many takes on Jung's theory, finding this particular metaperspective would not have been possible. Thanks to Judah Ben'Joshua, Sola Power, Laura Power, Melanie Ho, Gavin Sterley, Estellaleigh Franenberg, Beverly Barloff, and Nadine Nardi Davidson for their helpful and supportive feedback. Special thanks to Kris Kiler, who continually encouraged me to write this book, and Vicky Jo Varner, for her insightful feedback and many hours devoted to the editing process.

Contents

1. Being Yourself 1

2. Unfolding Your Potential 13

3. Immersing in the Present Context 23

4. Stabilizing with a Predictable Standard 39

5. Exploring the Emerging Patterns 55

6. Transforming with a Metaperspective 71

7. Measuring and Constructing for Progress 87

8. Gaining Leverage Using a Framework 103

9. Building Trust through Giving Relationships 119

10. Staying True to Who You Really Are 135

11. From Awareness to Action 151

12. Continuing Your Journey 171

Appendix—History of and Evidence for Cognitive Processes 183
Notes 197
Bibliography 199
About the Author 200

Being Yourself

The Eight Cognitive Processes Are Your Keys to Self-Leadership

Life can demand a lot if we want to be happy and successful. Wouldn't it be nice to know the keys to more insightful perception and wiser decision making? This guide honors your natural talents and helps you stretch yourself into new areas while keeping that sense of learning and wonder you had as a child. As you read, you will learn how to unlock the eight key cognitive processes—eight ways to find greater satisfaction in all that you do.

Exploring Cognitive Processes

Learning and growing involve new experiences, so let's start with an activity to exercise the mind.

Refer to the drawing below as you do the two activities that follow:

1. Look at the drawing. Notice the shapes, shadings, and placement of images on the page. Just allow your eyes to explore where they will. Now, what opportunities for action or tasks do you see in the drawing?

2. Why do you suppose apples were chosen as a stimulus to explore personal growth? Brainstorm as many ideas as you can. Now, what potential is there to use the ideas you have generated in some other part of your life?

These two activities exemplify cognitive processes we all use to some extent in daily life. The first activity asks you to look at the drawing in detail and see "what is." The scene suggested a course of action, such as picking the apples. The activity reflects what happens in real life: when we are highly attentive to our physical environment, we see and can act on the opportunities before us. The second activity asks you to imagine "what might be" and link your ideas to other situations. The activity reflects what happens in real life: when we are attentive to patterns and interactions, we can open ourselves up to new innovative possibilities.

Now reflect. Which activity was more fun? While you were trying each one, did you experience an increase or a decrease in energy level? Which activity felt more like how you do things? Asking questions like these is a first step to self-leadership.

The Essentials of Self-Leadership

Self-leadership takes three qualities:

1. Knowing and valuing your natural talents—what you like to do and are good at

2. Being aware of what you are not so good at or dislike, with a willingness to adapt or to accept challenges

3. Persevering with flexibility when you encounter obstacles and setbacks

Eight Keys

The following section summarizes the eight cognitive processes—your keys to self-leadership. Read and rate each key to pick out your strengths and areas to develop. Afterward, you can jump ahead to the pages indicated to start exploring. Each chapter on a cognitive process starts with detailed questions you can use to more fully assess yourself. Or you can continue this chapter and learn the theory behind each process and discover the hidden pattern that fits best for you. Knowing that pattern will unlock your potential.

IMMERSING IN THE PRESENT CONTEXT

Respond naturally to everything tangible you detect through your senses. Check what your gut instincts tell you. Test limits and take risks for big rewards.

NOT LIKE ME ○ ○ ○ ○ ○   A LOT LIKE ME ⟹ PAGE 23

STABILIZING WITH A PREDICTABLE STANDARD

Carefully compare a situation to the customary ways you've come to rely on. Check with past experiences. Stabilize the situation and invest for future security.

NOT LIKE ME ○ ○ ○ ○ ○   A LOT LIKE ME ⟹ PAGE 39

EXPLORING THE EMERGING PATTERNS

Wonder about patterns of interaction across various situations. Check what hypotheses fit best. Shift the dynamics of a situation and trust what emerges.

NOT LIKE ME ○ ○ ○ ○ ○   A LOT LIKE ME ⟹ PAGE 55

TRANSFORMING WITH A METAPERSPECTIVE

Withdraw from the world and focus your mind to receive an insight or realization. Check whether synergy results. Try out a realization to transform yourself.

NOT LIKE ME ○ ○ ○ ○ ○   A LOT LIKE ME ⟹ PAGE 71

MEASURING AND CONSTRUCTING FOR PROGRESS

Make decisions objectively based on evidence and measures. Check whether things function properly. Apply procedures to control events and achieve goals.

NOT LIKE ME ○ ○ ○ ○ ○   A LOT LIKE ME   ⇒   PAGE 87

GAINING LEVERAGE USING A FRAMEWORK

Detach yourself from a situation to study it from different angles and fit it to a theory, framework, or principle. Check this fit for accuracy. Use the leverage you gain to solve any problem.

NOT LIKE ME ○ ○ ○ ○ ○   A LOT LIKE ME   ⇒   PAGE 103

BUILDING TRUST THROUGH GIVING RELATIONSHIPS

Empathically respond to others' needs and take on their needs and values as your own. Check for respect and trust. Give and receive support to grow closer to people.

NOT LIKE ME ○ ○ ○ ○ ○   A LOT LIKE ME   ⇒   PAGE 119

STAYING TRUE TO WHO YOU REALLY ARE

Pay close attention to your personal identity, values, and beliefs. Check with your conscience before you act. Choose behavior congruent with what is important to you.

NOT LIKE ME ○ ○ ○ ○ ○   A LOT LIKE ME   ⇒   PAGE 135

Cracking the Cognitive Code

In the 1920s, Swiss psychiatrist Carl Jung observed eight "functions" of human nature—the eight cognitive processes that people use to gather information and make decisions. He described eight ways the mind relates to the world around it and to itself. Maybe we actively make decisions based on personal values—this involves talking with others and acting on our values, not just thinking about them. Or maybe we enjoy engaging the world around us directly through the five senses, trusting our gut instinct. We use the eight cognitive processes actively to get from one moment to the next within the larger systems of life—our environment, our use of tools, our relationships with other people, and our culture.

An Inner and an Outer World

Jung noticed that people can orient themselves to the outside world (extraverting). This is the world of people, places, objects, and actions. Alternatively, people can orient themselves to the world inside themselves (introverting). This is the world of thoughts, feelings, memories, and imagination. Jung believed that people have a preference that influences their behavior, and the difference between the two orientations lies in where we focus and recharge our energy. Also, extraverting often means initiating activities and interactions, while introverting means waiting and responding.

Four Basic Processes

Jung also identified four basic processes. A code letter stands for each process. In any situation, we can focus our attention using either of the following perceiving processes:

- Sensing (S)—tangible, experiential awareness
- Intuiting (N)—symbolic, conceptual awareness

Also, we can make decisions and organize using either of the following judging processes:

- Thinking (T)—objective criteria, logical reasoning, and impersonal principles
- Feeling (F)—appropriateness, values, and importance or worth to self and others

Our smallest acts involve all four basic processes. All are needed, valuable, and available to everyone.

A Total of Eight Processes

We can use each of the four basic processes in either the external world (extraverting) or the internal world (introverting). Thus we use a total of eight processes.

A common notation scheme is used to name the processes: the capital letter that stands for the process (S, N, T, or F) plus a lowercase e or i to indicate the orientation. For example, Se means extraverted Sensing, or Sensing awareness of the outer world; Fi means introverted Feeling, or Feeling evaluation made quietly within oneself.

The self-rating process you did earlier (pages 3–4) gave a sense of the eight processes. Here they are again, organized in terms of the underlying theory.

TABLE 1.1: A quick look at the eight cognitive processes

Extraverting	Introverting
Perceiving—how we focus attention	
Extraverted Sensing (Se) Take tangible action relevant to the moment and current context.	**Introverted Sensing (Si)** Compare something to expected details and reliable precedents.
Extraverted Intuiting (Ne) Explore imaginative potential possibilities as they emerge.	**Introverted Intuiting (Ni)** Realize a greater level of awareness to transform who you are and how you think.
Judging—how we make decisions	
Extraverted Thinking (Te) Create structure, reason by measures and evidence, and implement plans.	**Introverted Thinking (Ti)** Analyze a problem using a framework, and find an angle or leverage by which to solve it.
Extraverted Feeling (Fe) Connect with people by sharing values and taking on their needs as yours.	**Introverted Feeling (Fi)** Choose and stick to what you believe is congruent with your personal identity.

You Already Have Two Keys to Self-Leadership

Jung observed that everyone has potential access to all eight cognitive processes but that we each prefer one as dominant—playing a lead role—with a second process playing a support role. These two preferred cognitive processes are your first two keys to self-leadership.

An everyday metaphor is hammering a nail: our lead hand uses the hammer while our other hand holds the nail in place.

Sign your name here

_____

Now sign your name again using your other hand:

_____

Did you notice that writing with your dominant hand took little effort and that more concentration was required with the other hand? Similarly, you prefer some cognitive processes; and just as you can use your nonpreferred hand, you can and do engage all eight cognitive processes at different times and levels of proficiency.

Our two preferred processes allow us to do perceiving and judging, introverting and extraverting. We seem to have a built-in preference for one of the four perceiving processes and one of the four judging processes. Similarly, we tend to use one of our two preferred processes for introverting and the other for extraverting. Maybe you prefer introverted Intuiting in a lead role with extraverted Feeling in a support role, or maybe you prefer extraverted Sensing in a lead role with introverted Thinking in a support role. Or maybe you prefer some other pairing. These pairings tap into sixteen possible patterns. These will be shown in more detail in the next few pages.

Sixteen Type Patterns

Jung's ideas became popular through the work of Isabel Myers and David Keirsey. You may be familiar with the Myers-Briggs Type Indicator® (MBTI®) questionnaire, among other questionnaires, which provides a four-letter personality type code (ESTJ, INFP, etc.) that helps people discover which of sixteen personality type patterns fits them best. Your four-letter code represents your two preferred processes. Knowing your

TABLE 1.2 Sixteen personality type patterns

Foreseer Developer (INFJ)	Harmonizer Clarifier (INFP)
Prefer Introverted Intuiting—Realize a greater level of awareness to transform yourself. Extraverted Feeling—Connect with people by sharing values and taking on their needs as yours. *Develop*—Introverted Thinking, Extraverted Sensing, and Introverted Feeling.	*Prefer* Introverted Feeling—Choose and stick to what you believe is congruent with your personal identity. Extraverted Intuiting—Flow with imaginative potential possibilities as they emerge. *Develop*—Introverted Sensing, Extraverted Thinking, and Introverted Intuiting.
Envisioner Mentor (ENFJ)	Discoverer Advocate (ENFP)
Prefer Extraverted Feeling—Connect with people by sharing values and taking on their needs as yours. Introverted Intuiting—Realize a greater level of awareness to transform yourself. *Develop*—Extraverted Sensing, Introverted Thinking, and Extraverted Intuiting.	*Prefer* Extraverted Intuiting—Flow with imaginative potential possibilities as they emerge. Introverted Feeling—Choose and stick to what you believe is congruent with your personal identity. *Develop*—Extraverted Thinking, Introverted Sensing, and Extraverted Feeling.
Conceptualizer Director (INTJ)	Designer Theorizer (INTP)
Prefer Introverted Intuiting—Realize a greater level of awareness to transform yourself. Extraverted Thinking—Create structures, reason by measures and evidence, and implement plans. *Develop*—Introverted Feeling, Extraverted Sensing, and Introverted Thinking.	*Prefer* Introverted Thinking—Analyze a problem using a framework, and find an angle or leverage by which to solve it. Extraverted Intuiting—Flow with imaginative potential possibilities as they emerge. *Develop*—Introverted Sensing, Extraverted Feeling, and Introverted Intuiting.
Strategist Mobilizer (ENTJ)	Explorer Inventor (ENTP)
Prefer Extraverted Thinking—Create structures, reason by measures and evidence, and implement plans. Introverted Intuiting—Realize a greater level of awareness to transform yourself. *Develop*—Extraverted Sensing, Introverted Feeling, and Extraverted Intuiting.	*Prefer* Extraverted Intuiting—Flow with imaginative potential possibilities as they emerge. Introverted Thinking—Analyze a problem using a framework, and find an angle or leverage by which to solve it. *Develop*—Extraverted Feeling, Introverted Sensing, and Extraverted Thinking.

Planner Inspector (ISTJ)	Protector Supporter (ISFJ)
Prefer Introverted Sensing—Compare something to expected details and reliable precedents. Extraverted Thinking—Create structures, reason by measures and evidence, and implement plans. **Develop**—Introverted Feeling, Extraverted Intuiting, and Introverted Thinking.	**Prefer** Introverted Sensing—Compare something to expected details and reliable precedents. Extraverted Feeling—Connect with people by sharing values and taking on their needs as yours. **Develop**—Introverted Thinking, Extraverted Intuiting, and Introverted Feeling.
Implementor Supervisor (ESTJ)	Facilitator Caretaker (ESFJ)
Prefer Extraverted Thinking—Create structures, reason by measures and evidence, and implement plans. Introverted Sensing—Compare something to expected details and reliable precedents. **Develop**—Extraverted Intuiting, Introverted Feeling, and Extraverted Sensing.	**Prefer** Extraverted Feeling—Connect with people by sharing values and taking on their needs as yours. Introverted Sensing—Compare something to expected details and reliable precedents. **Develop**—Extraverted Intuiting, Introverted Thinking, and Extraverted Sensing.
Analyzer Operator (ISTP)	Composer Producer (ISFP)
Prefer Introverted Thinking—Analyze a problem using a framework, and find an angle or leverage by which to solve it. Extraverted Sensing—Take tangible action relevant to the moment and current context. **Develop**—Introverted Intuiting, Extraverted Feeling, and Introverted Sensing.	**Prefer** Introverted Feeling—Choose and stick to what you believe is congruent with your personal identity. Extraverted Sensing—Take tangible action relevant to the moment and current context. **Develop**—Introverted Intuiting, Extraverted Thinking, and Introverted Sensing.
Promoter Executer (ESTP)	Motivator Presenter (ESFP)
Prefer Extraverted Sensing—Take tangible action relevant to the moment and current context. Introverted Thinking—Analyze a problem using a framework, and find an angle or leverage by which to solve it. **Develop**—Extraverted Feeling, Introverted Intuiting, and Extraverted Thinking.	**Prefer** Extraverted Sensing—Take tangible action relevant to the moment and current context. Introverted Feeling—Choose and stick to what you believe is congruent with your personal identity. **Develop**—Extraverted Thinking, Introverted Intuiting, and Extraverted Feeling.

best fit type can help you identify strengths and options for development. The table "Sixteen Personality Type Patterns" on the previous two pages includes the four-letter type codes for readers familiar with that construct (see the appendix for more information). Keep your mind open to discovering your best fit type.

A Map to More Keys

You can realize your potential for self-leadership by understanding and practicing the cognitive processes. But which cognitive processes are most practical or appropriate to explore and develop first? Use the table on the previous two pages to decide.

First, use the table to locate which processes you prefer most. As you explore, consider this: noticing our own preferences is like noticing the air we breathe. Our preferences are ever-present, perhaps taken for granted or unnoticed. Moreover, "preference" does not mean "perfectly adept." Nor does lack of preference mean "can't use." Preference promotes use, and we need full mature use for peak performance.

Second, for each personality type pattern, the table suggests three processes to develop as good ways to unlock your potential. These three help balance and expand upon your existing gifts without competing with or undermining them. Depending on your age and life experience, you may or may not have already developed these.

Finally, consider exploring and developing all eight to include them in your life in some way.

Now What?

You have been introduced to the basic tools with which to start the rest of your journey. Now you will see when and how to use them.

Chapter 2, "Unfolding Your Potential," explores lifelong development. With maturity, we discover new aspects of our preferred processes, use them together in new ways, and develop our nonpreferred processes.

Chapters 3 through 10 take you through the eight cognitive processes in detail. Each chapter includes the following tools:
- A cartoon—enjoy a lighthearted introduction to evoke the cognitive processes.

- Benefits for self-leadership—read four tangible reasons to develop the process.
- Self-assessment—understand your level of development for the process and how you are using it with other processes.
- An explanation of the process—understand how it works cognitively.
- Many best-use activities—see what the process looks like in action and learn ways you can start using it.
- Case studies—read examples of the process in use.
- Tips—learn the process from those who already use it well.
- A detailed guide—develop and include the process in your life.

Chapter 11, "From Awareness to Action," offers a variety of general activities, to do alone or with others, that have proven effective in facilitating self-leadership.

Chapter 12, "Continuing Your Journey," includes numerous tips for honing your observational skills. Read this chapter to truly start mastering the concepts so you can apply them more effectively.

The appendix summarizes the history of psychological type and gives statistical results from a research study. What you're doing has empirical validation.

Have fun!

When you know who you are you are freer to be who you are not.
Linda V. Berens

Unfolding Your Potential

Understanding Lifelong Cognitive Development

When we walk down the street, we use more than our feet. We look around, avoid obstacles, and maybe chat with a friend or daydream. Similarly, when we talk about a cognitive process, we are focusing on one aspect of who we are, but there is a bigger picture, a broader pattern. A big part of who we are is genetic. Ongoing demands of life and upbringing also shape how our innate potential unfolds. The result is a whole self—variously called our psyche, our personality, or our developed self. In the following pages we will explore the story of lifelong development.

We grow from innate potential.

The achievement of personality means nothing less than the optimum development of the whole individual human being.
Carl Jung

Your Lead Process

Our lead (preferred) cognitive process is normally the one we trust, use the most, and have the greatest skill with, having developed it since childhood. Like right- and left-handedness, our lead process seems to be innate. We actively search for ways to use our preferences, so at the very least, moderate development is likely. You know your lead process because it is the one you've always had and the one you can't live without.

Jane's Story

At age thirty-five Jane is very much like she was at age seven, but more developed. Her basic personality was present early on, and she is still discovering and developing new aspects of herself all the time from her life experiences. When she was seven, she often helped take care of her classmates to be supportive of her second-grade teacher. She remembers empathizing when the teacher felt overwhelmed by a huge class. Today Jane is a high-level manager working closely with executives to facilitate company relations. These two activities are uncannily similar and but one example of many in her life. The cognitive processes she uses now are also similar to those she used as a child. Her basic personality has not changed. She engaged in extraverted Feeling and introverted Sensing when she was seven; today her use of these two processes is much more sophisticated, and it is informed by other processes, often with synergistic results.

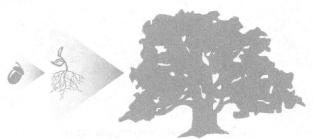

Growth is an ongoing organic process.

Growing from a Core Self

Jane's experience is unsurprising since human beings are living systems. We develop organically—often gradually, perhaps in punctuated leaps, but always as a whole. The life cycle of a tree is a metaphor for this wholeness in development. Each stage of the life cycle reflects something unique about the tree at that time.

TABLE 2.1: Stages of the life cycle

Stage	Tree	The Tree's Special Qualities	Person
0	Seed	Potential tree coded for development	Embryo
1	Sprout	Connected to and nourished by the seed	Child
2	Sapling	Still soft, pliable, and easily shaped by the environment (can be influenced to grow in a certain way)	Youth
3	Adult	Bears fruit and stays hearty when environment changes	Adult
4	Mature	Shows character, has history and a role (meaning and purpose) in its environment, and has withstood the tests of time	Senior

The stages in the table are not absolute. There is a specific day when a tree bears its first fruit but that fruit is usually small and inedible. A mature tree with plentiful, tasty fruit takes years to develop. Also notice that the tree does not turn into a different kind of tree over time. It is the same entity it was as a seed, and it is shaped by its environment and genetic plan with each passing year.

Following this metaphor, a pattern of cognitive growth emerges in people—each process relating to all the others and to where we are in our environment. This whole pattern is present and operating ("metabolizing") from the start. With experience and resources we mature as a whole. And as we mature, each cognitive process plays out in new ways.

TABLE 2.2: Stages of the life cycle and use of a cognitive process

Stage	Our Experience and Use of a Cognitive Process
0	No awareness or conscious use
1	Basic use: We passively experience a process in its instinctual or basic form; we try to block out, explore, or fixate on the experience; use is rough or childlike.
2	Specialized use: We accept and follow a limited social or cultural version of the process; it shapes our lives and may "have us in its grasp"; use is rigid or adolescent. Often we use it in the service of other processes.
3	Advanced use: We grasp the process in its many forms; we question, alter, and personalize it and make it our own, as a tool with many options; use is complex and flexible.
4	Integrated use: We integrate the process, now highly sophisticated, with the rest of who we are, and we use it to contribute to the world; use is purposeful, creative, and generative.

Basic and Advanced Use

Each cognitive process can be engaged in a basic, unsophisticated way. For example, basic extraverted Sensing means gathering information using the five senses, and basic introverted Thinking means making decisions based on a scientific principle we have been taught. Everyone can engage all eight processes in a basic way as part of our human heritage.

We can engage our preferred processes in more developed, sophisticated ways. For example, only a few of us have the heightened sensory awareness and superb bodily coordination to jump between moving trains or to paint or sculpt like Michelangelo. Advanced use comes from an innate preference plus lifelong growth and practice. Because life history plays a major role, advanced use shows itself differently from person to person. One person jumps trains; another is a quick-acting entrepreneur. Advanced use includes consciously shaping, modifying, and intervening in how we use the process.

As you explore and develop the cognitive processes, remember that basic does not mean "lesser" and advanced does not always mean "skilled." Our use of a process may be awkward as we keep revisiting and developing it in new ways. Overengaging or rigidly engaging a process are also typical as we develop. Overengaging is useful in discovering just what a process can and cannot do for us, and some rigid use serves as practice. Also, as you develop some processes you may necessarily neglect others until a later time.

Try to maintain some basic use of all eight cognitive processes since underuse leads to "blind spots" and possibly major mistakes.

EXAMPLE: EXTRAVERTED SENSING

Basic use of extraverted Sensing means perceiving tangible data through the five senses. At the other end of the developmental spectrum, people who lead with mature extraverted Sensing actively move and engage the world and smoothly make an impact. They are quick yet relaxed, unassuming yet very effective. So what lies between each end of the spectrum?

People often start exploring extraverted Sensing by merging with the moment. They let the tangible, immediate context and their instinctual impulses guide their actions. This is more sophisticated than just taking in data, but it is still passive use. We are driven or shaped by what is given (the context and our impulses). The process can quickly take control of us and take us where it will. For many people who prefer some other process, the story ends here.

People who continue to develop extraverted Sensing take ownership of the process and gain comfort from it. Using it becomes a vital aspect of who they are. They engage the environment and act quickly with ease and enjoyment but do not lose themselves in it. They play music because they enjoy playing, not because they must practice; and they set no standards or goals, yet they do things that get results. At some point they are ready to engage the process in its most mature form—pulling off results and spurring action from others simply by making their presence felt.

The Evidence for Cognitive Development

Research in human development suggests that cognitive processes unfold over time. For example, as children we develop the basic use of introverted Sensing, such as drawing on a simple sense of permanence to recognize that our parents will return, even if they leave us while we play or sleep. Later, some of us may start using introverted Sensing in an advanced way, with a deep understanding of and ability to foster what is reliable, familiar, and essentially permanent.

Psychologists distinguish between "having an idea" and "an idea having us." For example, we might follow a philosophical principle so rigidly that we lose our sense of personal choice and responsibility. In contrast, when we take hold of a process, we gain perspective and make it our own. Psychologists frequently observe clients experiencing this change. We might start out lacking awareness of a particular belief, then notice what impact the belief is having. Maybe we've been demanding that others be like us, or we've been trying very hard to be someone we're not, maybe trying to fit a societal value or parental expectation. Over time, we break free from the belief's hold and begin to internalize our own beliefs. We explore beliefs about beliefs! Eventually the circle may close as we find a way to live in peace with many beliefs in and around ourselves.

Environment—our role models and resources—strongly influences development. Consider what your parents' lead cognitive processes were and how growing up with those processes influenced you. We absorb a great deal from our parents, siblings, colleagues, and others—consciously or unconsciously. As children, a world rich in toys and tools affords us many opportunities to play, practice, and hone our skills. Some of this activity will not fit us well. A well-meaning parent might encourage a quiet, artistic child to be more practical. In other cases the benefit is indirect or will appear later; maybe a few practical experiences will make the child more ready for school. And sometimes we get to practice our natural talents abundantly. Also consider how your career path and long-term job demands have encouraged or discouraged certain processes.

Cognitive development also involves integrating—bringing together many aspects of ourselves into a sufficiently coherent whole. Brain research supports this observation. In childhood, isolated brain regions start developing, linking with each other here and there, each like a tree with roots spreading out and perhaps touching other trees' roots. Over time, these regions become more cohesive, forming a forestlike network of interrelated processes. Our mind thus begins to function more as a whole than as discrete modules. And as adults we may learn how to consciously encourage peak performance. A professional writer, for example, knows how to call upon his or her inner muse—a unique method that is likely a host of processes harnessed around an activity. The synergy that results from integration is exciting and highly productive.

Satisfying, healthy growth depends on environment.

Don't ask yourself what the world needs. Ask yourself what makes you come alive, and then go do that. Because what the world needs is people who have come alive.
Reverend Howard Thurman

Synergistic Use

When we experience moments of synergy, what is happening? Our preferences often indicate which cognitive processes will be easiest to use together, but much is possible.

Certain processes can be used together quite well, particularly when they play complementary roles. For example, introverted Thinking can be used smoothly with extraverted Sensing. We use one process to gather data and the other to evaluate. Even processes that seem unrelated can enhance our handling of situations. Using introverted Thinking with introverted Sensing might mean drawing upon a rich storehouse of specific past experiences to inform us of how well a management principle has fared or how it might be revised or what the historical roots and established thinking (the predictable standard) tell us of the subject.

Some processes are challenging to use together. When we use extraverted Intuiting, we draw on random outside information as we hypothesize about hidden patterns and dynamics. These patterns cross contexts. In contrast, when we use extraverted Sensing, we immerse ourselves in the current context and focus on direct experience and tangible data. Use is so different: do we immerse ourselves or do we split off? Using both processes at once is like trying to walk on the bottom of a swimming pool. Yet with these two processes we might use physical activity to facilitate a group dynamic or use a metaphor to better gauge the limits of actions we can take right now.

As a guideline, consider how much support or conflict comes from using two processes. A little conflict often leads to growth, but too much conflict creates a swamp that limits effectiveness.

Tandem Use[1]

We can develop and use processes that are "opposite" to our preferences to produce powerful results for ourselves and our organizations. Which processes are opposites?

- Extraverted Sensing and introverted Intuiting
- Introverted Sensing and extraverted Intuiting
- Extraverted Thinking and introverted Feeling
- Introverted Thinking and extraverted Feeling

Developing opposite processes is not fully under our conscious control, but exploring them is often very rewarding. They can play challenging or aspirational roles, and using them can bring stress relief and creative results. In particular, a powerful relationship called "tandem use" exists between a cognitive process and its opposite.

What is tandem use? Imagine a tandem bicycle with two riders. The front rider pedals and steers. The back rider just pedals. Without the front rider, we can't control where we are going. Without the back rider, pedaling is harder work. We could simply ride a one-person bicycle by ourselves, but then we miss out on doing something greater than ourselves.

For example, when we use introverted Thinking, we look inward to a logical framework and we observe only; we eschew opinions and others' subjective values. In apparent opposition to that, when we use extraverted Feeling, we reach outward to connect with people; we exchange values and take on other people's needs as our own. Yet with maturity we can use these two processes in tandem. We might draw on a theory of effective teamwork to make adjustments for the welfare of others or the good of the group. Applying universal principles of human and group behavior and intervening at key leverage points can help us manage people's divergent values, feelings, and opinions in a way that extraverted Feeling by itself might not. The U.S. Constitution exemplifies what happens when people draw upon principles like "a balance of powers" as part of creating a social contract by which everyone can get along together.

Not everyone has the chance to develop tandem use in a big way. But small opportunities arise, such as taking an observer role as a neutral party to solve a conflict between two friends.

Possible Misuse

Sometimes we use a process in rigid and dominating ways, either because of stress or because it's the only way we know in a particular situation. For example, using extraverted Sensing means having sensory awareness and acting in the present context, and it is possible to become hedonistic using this process. We might go through a spate of shopping or eating too much. Or we might avoid discussing anything not observable by the five senses. One antidote for this misuse is further development of the process. In this case, we remember to scope out the limits of a context—for example, how many calories we can eat—before following our impulses or taking a risk.

Other times misuse means not using a process when the situation calls for it, and we compensate by using another process. For example, we might wonder and hypothesize what's happening outside our house when all we need to do is look out the window. Similarly, because our gut instincts are an important source of information for our survival, ignoring an impulse might lead to physical harm. The antidote for this misuse involves asking ourselves which processes are better suited to a situation and remembering that all the processes have something to offer.

Growth follows the natural seasons of our lives, so remember to be patient with yourself as you discover effective ways to use each process.

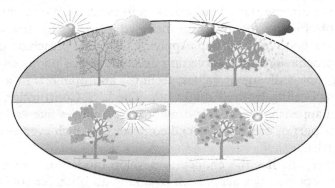

Growth follows the natural seasons of life.

There is no linear evolution; there is only a circumambulation of the self. Uniform development exists, at most only at the beginning; later, everything points toward the center.

Carl Jung

Maintaining Perspective

Our lead process remains the captain of our ship no matter how much developing we do. We use it in the background even when using other processes. Lead and supporting processes develop first, and each experience we have of nonpreferred processes is cause for celebration and a doorway to change.

Development often happens in the service of our preferred processes. Someone who prefers introverted Sensing might follow a mentor or guidebook to develop various cognitive processes because the culture he is most familiar and comfortable with values a standard of well-rounded development. Yet even as this person develops, he is still exercising his deep preference for introverted Sensing.

Eight processes with basic and advanced use plus synergy and tandem dynamics create a total of thirty-two categories. If we explore and develop three or four categories each decade, then it takes half a lifetime to experience even half our potential.

3

Immersing in the
Present Context

Understanding and Developing Extraverted Sensing

Benefits for Self-Leadership

As you develop extraverted Sensing, you will
- Feel greater confidence taking risks
- Experience heightened awareness of your physical environment
- Find it easier to do many activities simultaneously
- Enjoy more of life's pleasures

Assessing Current Development

Before continuing, check the phrases in the table that describe you well.

Part 1
☐ Instantly notice movement and impactful features in the environment.
☐ Freely follow your gut instincts and exciting physical impulses.
☐ Instantly read visible cues to see just how far you can go.
Part 2
☐ Quickly move to take advantage of immediate options for action.
☐ Easily get in synch physically with people and things around you.
Part 3
☐ Become totally absorbed as you move, touch, and see what's around you.
☐ Enjoy the thrill of action and physical experience in the present moment.
☐ Spur action and get results simply by making your presence felt.

Scoring: Assign one point to items in part 1, two points to items in part 2, and three points to items in part 3.

Total points: 5

A score above nine indicates a likely preference for extraverted Sensing. A score from four to nine indicates a possible supporting preference or development from life experience. A score below four suggests a lack of development.

Understanding How
Extraverted Sensing Works

At the core of extraverted Sensing is the present context. It's where we are, what we're doing, and who we're with right now. The present context is what is. It's tangible: it's what we see, hear, and feel. It's our options and our impulses for action. By staying with what is here and now, we expand our experience to everything we can sense and do in that context with all its richness, challenges, and exhilarating rewards. Nothing moves without our notice. We can try out everything. We may circulate in other contexts tomorrow, but heightening and shaping our experience of the moment demands that we stay with what is in front of us.

Best-Use Activities

What can we do in the present context? We can explore and familiarize ourselves with the context, with all its details and relevant facts, tools and actors, obstacles and pathways. We learn all the ins and outs the way a painter might know every brush and pigment or a salesperson every product and technique. We might want to move around to stay in touch and up to date with everything, perhaps often visiting associates or tracking our industry's daily buzz. With repeated exposure and interaction we know this context like the back of our hand and can deal with whatever comes up.

Our instincts, impulses, and gut reactions are aroused as we engage with the environment. What looks nice? We notice features like color intensity, highlights and textures, layering and curvature. What tastes, feels, smells, and sounds good? What's moving, how fast is it going, and where is it headed? We might follow our instincts, perhaps moving all over the place or quietly savoring something. Our natural responses often evoke the same responses in others as we enjoy activities and create new experiences with the people around us. Often this involves matching another's pace and style, whether dancing with a partner, negotiating a deal, or studying animals in their habitat. This is easier if we feel chemistry between ourselves and the other person (or the animal).

We can become one with a context, getting in synch with the flow of events as we take in everything that is around us. This "being in the zone" allows multisensory multitasking—we can perform many actions skillfully at once. Anything out of context chafes us and we may push it away. If we're enjoying the high point of artistic motivation or a business negotiation and someone is insisting on a heated debate, our desire might be for that person to go away. We want to enjoy and

FIG. 3.1. Cognitive snapshot of extraverted sensing

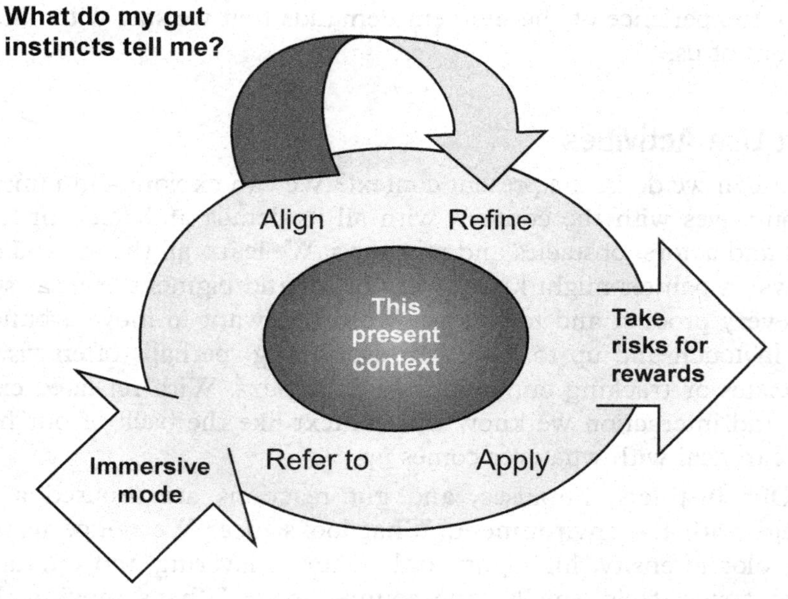

At the core of extraverted Sensing is the present context—where we are and what we're doing right now. When we go into an immersive mode, we allow ourselves to respond naturally to everything we detect through our senses. We can refer to, align, refine, and interact with the present context. Interacting often means testing limits and taking risks to gain rewards. We reflect on the present context by asking, what do my gut instincts tell me?

take advantage of what's going on right now because tomorrow it will be gone. If someone knows us well from one context, that person may still be surprised when meeting us in another context, where we're using different tools and drawing on a different knowledge base.

Having tools and equipment allows us to interact with the present context. Knowing how to use these tools and equipment and improvise new ones is useful. A tool might be a guitar, a computer, or a mental model. We play with it to learn all the ways it can be used. Abstraction is accepted if it can be applied, and hidden patterns like peoples' motives are interesting so long as they relate to the present moment.

Immersing ourselves includes testing limits to gauge the scope of things and to find out what we're capable of. Are we taking advantage of all the resources and options right in front of us? Options might be actions to take, signals with which to arouse a response from others, people to interact with, ideas and tools that advance us, or challenges to set or accept. Someone winks at us. Let's respond! To others our actions can look like risk taking, but we know the situation and trust our senses and our gut feel. We try our best and keep our eyes open. As we go with our instincts we stay with a context or leave it.

Those who prefer extraverted Sensing rely on a freedom to respond instinctively, and they use their keen senses and instincts to navigate life and make sense of all aspects of living.

Mind-Set and Feedback

Using extraverted Sensing requires that we let go of artificial inhibitions to become one with a context by following our instincts and merging with it. The surfer "becomes" the wave. The politician becomes the negotiation. The musician becomes the instrument and music. To detach ourselves and wonder about hypotheticals or to merely talk or daydream is to miss what we can do now. Engaging with the contexts we move through can make life richly enjoyable and rewarding.

When immersing ourselves, listening to our gut-level responses may keep us in place or lead us to new contexts, activities, and experiences. When our instincts are satisfied, we have a tremendous feeling of ease and success.

Possible Misuses

Sometimes use of the extraverted Sensing process becomes rigid and dominating because of stress or because it is used without skill and without other processes to balance it. When this occurs, we may

- Become hedonistic and overly self-indulgent; for example, shopping or eating too much
- Feel plagued by unwanted impulses that overwhelm will power
- Act in a way that others perceive as physically dangerous, wild, or self-destructive
- Avoid discussing anything not tangible to the five senses or in the here and now
- Overly limit ourselves to repeating the experiences of a single context

Case Studies

The following vignettes illustrate extraverted Sensing. The first is an everyday personal situation and the second is an organizational situation that includes other processes.

Case A

As Sandy is helping a friend sign out from the hospital, she spots someone in a wheelchair in a precarious position on the sidewalk. She can tell what's going to happen by the slight way the chair is tipping and the expression of imbalance on the man's face. She rushes over and catches the chair before her friend is aware anything is happening.
Later at work, someone comes to Sandy for help. "Somehow this slipped past my team and the deadline is this afternoon. Can you help?" Everyone knows she's good in a crisis. She asks the team members a few key questions to learn what kind of outcome they want and what the parameters are. There is a bureaucratic obstacle, but Sandy knows just whom to talk to in every department to sidestep such obstacles. She finds the challenges exhilarating.

Case B

James presently enjoys running a small business of forty employees. Being in charge allows him to respond freely to opportunities that present themselves. He is constantly scanning the trade magazines and attending networking events to keep tabs on what's going on. Because he is so attuned to what's coming up and sees how well customers respond to his colorful and interactive products, he has been able to transform the company from a  small garage operation just a couple of years ago to its current size. He foresaw how his products could impact people. He's taken what some people call risks, without experiencing any real problems. Putting profits back into the business has meant slow rewards at times, but his gut instinct is to keep trying out things until the company catches a big break.

Perspective Shifting

Here are some suggestions for how to communicate with, learn from, and influence someone who is using extraverted Sensing.

- **Communicating to Build Rapport**
  - It's likely you and the other person share the same current context. If you don't, ask questions. Where is that person's activity taking place? He or she may refer to a place, activity, or subculture—the law firm, surfing, or the art world. Use that person's terms when you converse.
  - To gauge how the person feels about the current context, ask if he or she feels challenged and is having fun, or if he or she feels bored or outclassed. Use the language of the person's context if you know it, or use everyday terms if you don't.

- **Learning to Build New Skills**
  - Find out about the present context. Who's who, what's what, and what options for actions and activities are available? Don't ask all these questions at once; do some activities to find out some of the answers. You'll probably hear about what's happening now.

• Ask the person to describe what aspects of the current context are the most fun or challenging (risky). What visible clues signal tools for this person to use or actions to take for the greatest payoff? What visible clues indicate to this person that he or she is about to go too far? When is teamwork best? After actions are taken, what fallout results? For example, ask which employees tend to be most disgruntled after company crises are dealt with.

• **Influencing for Best Use**
  • What kind of impact is the person having on the context? Listen for negative as well as positive effects.
  • Ask how much the person has been able to go into an immersive mode and what he or she currently feels restrained from doing. If this person could have more freedom in one area, what would that area be?

• **Helping to Discover New Outcomes**
  • Ask the other person whether the present context is as rewarding as it could be. That is, considering the work the person does, the talents he or she comes with, and the risks he or she takes, is this person satisfied with his or her current level of success?
  • If the person is dissatisfied, is there a totally different context where this person could make an impact? (The person may not know what that new context might be.)

There is always more to be experienced,
and opportunities don't last.

Developing Extraverted Sensing

The following exercises will help you develop the extraverted Sensing process. Get your self-assessment score from the beginning of this chapter and then set your starting point using the chart below.

If you scored	Then start with
0–3	The Introductory Exercises
4–9	The Basic Exercises
10+	The Advanced Exercises

As you work through the coming exercises, you may find some are particularly challenging. Include all the following steps to get more satisfying use of this process:

1. To access the process in the most effective way, go into an instinctive, immersive mode. (See pages 166–167 to enter this mode.)

2. Access the core of the process: identify the present context and assess where you can experience a success or reward.

3. Engage in best-use activities, such as watching for features and movement that get your attention and testing the limits of what you can do.

4. Try for a desired outcome by taking a risk to experience the reward.

5. Get feedback and calibrate: observe your gut response to the present context and enjoyment of a payoff.

6. Integrate your use of extraverted Sensing with other cognitive processes (usually introverted Thinking or introverted Feeling).

As you develop this process, you'll be able to engage these steps all at once for increasingly coordinated and smooth use.

Introductory Exercises

Here are some brief exercises to help you get comfortable immersing yourself in the moment and taking action by following your instincts.

FOLLOW SENSORY DATA

Observe the physical environment around you. Let your attention be drawn to what's beautiful, what's in motion, or what is otherwise captivating to your senses. Now focus inside your body and notice impulses. (Do you want to smell the beautiful flower or run your finger over the rough texture?) What do you want to do right now?

IDENTIFY RISKS AND LIMITS

Look around for visible cues to the limits of what you can safely get away with. In sports, this might be an opening to pass or score. Let the situation drive what you can do. Put aside experience, imagination, values, and reasoning. What feels like an option or a risk and what are you willing to try? This may involve asking, will others be physically injured by this? or what might I lose permanently? Any and all actions within these limits are options!

SEIZE A MOMENT

Give yourself permission to act at a moment's notice and react immediately (without censoring yourself) to whatever impulse or option comes. You've explored risk limits, so nothing dangerous will happen! As soon as an action offers itself, do it. Act even if doing so preempts a current response to a previous cue or interrupts what someone is doing. This is disarming to some extent. However, this is how you can make an impact.

Basic Exercises

These exercises will help you get comfortable immersing yourself in an entire context, from getting the right equipment to learning the local culture and staying in the context.

LOCATE A CONTEXT

Choose a physical or artistic activity that has a culture around it, preferably with a friend who already participates. Surfers, painters, gardeners—these people spend time together, do an activity, and share a culture. An activity is action or movement that engages the senses. It might involve exercise, your health and body, nature, the arts, a craft, or sports. People who prefer the extraverted Sensing cognitive process aren't limited to these activities, but it's usually best to start here.

FAMILIARIZE YOURSELF WITH THE CONTEXT

Learn all aspects of the context you've chosen. What is it about? What can you do? What tools are popular? What are common alternatives? Who is noteworthy or popular? What social rules are involved? You can learn some aspects by reading magazines and surfing the Web, but the most direct path is learning by the motto "Ninety percent of life is showing up." You don't need to learn how to do everything; just gather as much knowledge as possible so that when you're in the context you follow what's going on.

GET APPROPRIATE EQUIPMENT

Many activities require equipment. Baseball requires a baseball and bat, a mitt, and a place to play. A regular meeting place is part of your equipment. Being welcomed into a group also requires the right clothes. If you're unsure about quality or brand, get the help of a friend already involved in the activity. Modest equipment is best. The activity isn't about the equipment; it's about the experience. Also, be open to improvising equipment as the opportunity arises.

TRY OUT THE EQUIPMENT

Touch the equipment, hold it in various positions, and try it out in different ways. Acclimate your muscles, hands, eyes, and mind to using these tools quickly and smoothly. If one way doesn't feel right, then keep trying to find a way that does. Find the fit that feels right to you to better use the tool at a moment's notice or to use multiple tools at once.

LEARN THE CULTURE

Every context has a lingo, a manner, and culture. Do not force yourself to adopt the culture or wear something that doesn't suit you. A "wannabe" can be an object of ridicule. Simply remain open to absorbing what comes up. You will absorb much of the culture just by being around others. Eventually, you will assume the culture naturally.

NOTICE STANDOUT FEATURES

Practice pursuing options as they come up in front of you. That is, keep your five senses constantly on the lookout for cues or features—facial expressions, clothing colors, and so on—that stand out. Features may stand out because they push the context to its limits: "Wow! That's not just a bike—it's the coolest bike!" Or they function but don't match the context: "What's that? Wearing PJs while biking?" You notice these standouts because you have been immersing yourself in the context. You may also notice them because other people in your context notice them. By noticing and reacting together, you build a cohesive group that shares the context and develop a sense of fraternity that is necessary to a team.

IMMERSE YOURSELF

Take in all the rich detail of the tools and environment around you—colors, shading, brightness, textures, gradients, granularity. Don't compare or analyze; just see the richness. To heighten this effect, do some deep relaxation or heavy exercise and then open your eyes and look around. Everything will seem more vibrant and real.

STAY IN THE CONTEXT

Staying in the context is particularly challenging for those who prefer extraverted Intuiting. Practice staying relevant to the context. When you go off on a tangent or bring in outside contexts, you distance yourself from the context and ruin the experience of using this process for everyone else.

ADJUST THE CONTEXT TO YOUR COMFORT

Pay attention to your body and your senses in this moment and respond. For example, if music is too loud for you right now, then turn it down to a volume that's just right. This process is about the here and now, not what you're accustomed to, which is based on the past and other contexts. Tomorrow your body and mind may respond differently, and a different setting will be more pleasing. If you aren't comfortable, your enjoyment of activities and your performance will be lower, and interactions with others will be harder, as they are when the ambient music is so loud that no one can hear each other. Practice paying attention to your body's desire to sleep or eat, and act on these internal drives. Again, this isn't about what you're accustomed to. It's about letting your senses decide.

Advanced Exercises

These exercises will help you hone your basic use of the extraverted Sensing process and develop some advanced use. Learn to take a more active role in creating and maintaining the present context.

KEEP CIRCULATING AND VARYING

The local environment usually grows stale after a while, so keep circulating in the context you have chosen. This can mean moving physically to a new location or trying a new group of people with whom to do your activity. Or it can mean varying what you are working on—for example, moving around elements of an artistic project. Keep varying, moving, and circulating at a smooth pace—not too much, only a little bit at a time. Otherwise, you will run out of options and circulate yourself right out of the context. Varying also plays an aesthetic role: pay attention to each small variation until you find the one that feels just right.

LEARN THE VISIBLE CUES

Watch the forms communication takes between people. Visible cues include facial expressions, postures, and gestures. A slight smile, a wink, open or closed eyes during a hug—these are tangible signs of the motivation behind communication. Some will be context specific—a unique team handshake, for example. Most will be common and natural, preferably not overdone. How people respond to these visible cues helps indicate who's fully accepted, who's not fully accepted, who feels free to behave naturally and not hide anything, and so on.

FOLLOW WHERE OTHERS LOOK

Pay attention to how others experience the present context. What cues, limits, and risks do they see? Follow their eyes. What do they look at? What are they looking at when their bodies tense, relax, or become energized? What facial expressions appear as they look at or engage a person, tool, or activity? How people carry themselves is informative about their overall confidence level.

TRY OUT INTERACTIONS

Entice others to join you by actively sending visible cues. You know these cues because you've become intimately familiar with the context. A cue is an invitation and needs to be sent only once, with perhaps a reminder just before the option expires. If the cue evokes a response, then pursue the joint activity. For example, if you feel ready to challenge the lead member of an opposing team, send one cue. If there's no response, wait for another time.

CREATE A PERSONAL STYLE

Everything you wear, say, do, and think should enhance who you are personally. If wearing a black suit enhances who you are, then wear that. Or maybe baggy jeans enhance who you are because you feel more comfortable in them. Similarly choose your tools, words, and thoughts. You can enhance your style by matching striking elements, such as a stripe of shoe color with a shirt color. Ideally, this match is perfect and rare; people wonder where you got it or where you learned it.

CULTIVATE GRACE, ENERGY, AND SMOOTHNESS

In each moment, imagine you are on camera in a movie. Do you want to be seen moving awkwardly or smoothly? Physical grace requires a strong, energetic, and balanced body as well as conscious attention to how your style may affect others. Finding ways to healthfully sustain your energy is vital to performing well. You can energize yourself through progressive sensory stimulation. For example, if you are tired you might listen to soft music, then more engaging music, then yet faster and more rhythmic sounds. Allow the power of the senses to enliven your step.

FIND YOUR HIGH POINT ZONE

Runners often describe an adrenaline high that carries them past exhaustion into a second wind. This is more than an energy boost. In this zone we can accomplish tremendous feats not otherwise possible. This zone is about hitting a stride that carries us. Everything vanishes but what's before us. We may feel extremely energized, body and mind as one. Similar to the runner, the artist's eye, mind, hand, and canvas become one. Sights, sounds, and other sensory data are incredibly vibrant and intense, and there is a continuous physical flowing, staying with the present. Draw upon everything you've learned to find and stay in your zone. With practice, you'll be able to engage in multiple actions and tools at the same time and accomplish more than you could have imagined.

KEEP PLAYING AND TESTING LIMITS

Continuously toy with how you use your equipment and how you engage in the activities you do. Keep varying a little at a time until you find a trick—an impressive way of doing what you do that leaves people wondering how you do it. The trick might be one that experts use or one you've discovered yourself. Slight modifications to your tools can allow for entirely new tricks. Overall, the environment around you, the people and tools in it, and what you are capable of are forever evolving and varying from day to day. Keep looking for and testing limits. Trust experience as your teacher.

SET UP SITUATIONS

Creating experiences involves setting up equipment and options for the team, not just for yourself, beforehand. It is fine to go slowly. Don't force, rush, or overplan because you'll find fun in building and releasing the expectations. Make the resources easily accessible and ready to use. Relax and enjoy the setting-up process, keep your eyes open for options, and keep varying and adapting what you do.

BECOME ONE WITH THE CONTEXT

In baseball, unless you want to strike out, you keep your eyes on the ball. When body-surfing, you become one with the wave. When we are in our high point zone, we "forget ourselves" and are no longer separate from the context. At times you may find yourself becoming one with the context as a whole—it becomes your way of being in the world. When this happens, you will be able to engage the present context in multiple ways at once for an incredibly impressive impact on others.

4

Stabilizing with a Predictable Standard

Understanding and Developing Introverted Sensing

Benefits for Self-Leadership

As you develop introverted Sensing, you will
- Feel a more solid connection to your roots
- Have practical knowledge to navigate life's many traditions and institutions
- Accumulate a thorough storehouse of experiences to draw on
- Be more comfortable and secure

Assessing Current Development

Before continuing, check the phrases in the table that describe you well.

Part 1
☐ Follow the work, ideas, and example of others who have come before you.
☐ Notice whether the details in front of you match what you are accustomed to.
☐ Review a lot of information over time to confirm a customary standard.

Part 2
☐ Feel inclined to put a stop to something new to your experience.
☐ Point out discrepancies between how things are and the way they have always been.

Part 3
☐ In emergencies, trust solutions that have stabilized the situation in the past.
☐ Compare an experience against a storehouse of familiar experiences to find what's reliable.
☐ Perform the same regular work or activity every day at an even, comfortable pace.

Scoring: Assign one point to items in part 1, two points to items in part 2, and three points to items in part 3.

Total points:

A score above nine indicates a likely preference for introverted Sensing. A score from four to nine indicates a possible supporting preference or development from life experience. A score below four suggests a lack of development.

Understanding How Introverted Sensing Works

At the core of introverted Sensing is a predictable standard—typically, a convention, historical practice, or tradition. It is what is most familiar to us, what we know and rely on. Based on its constancy, it may surely serve us well. A predictable standard might be a time-honored brand, a rock-solid relationship, a familiar furrowed brow, a team process that consistently works, or an enjoyable pastime. A standard may also be a form of government or a cherished cultural tradition or institution that has held steadfast for a group, for a culture, or for all people everywhere.

Best-Use Activities

What can we do with a predictable standard? We can compare how things are now with the standard we are familiar with. This often involves recalling past details, guidelines, events, and reactions, with expectations of what is meant to happen. Does our restaurant meal match our prior experience with this dish? How does it compare to Mom's standard? What ingredients are necessary to make it more like what we know? Comparisons like these require a large storehouse of specific, rich experiences to draw on, and when we perceive that something doesn't match, we may feel uncomfortable.

In order to be sure of a standard, we might seek to clarify what it means officially. So we need well-educated experts and historians and a reliable memory for details. Since we don't want to distort a convention or tradition and risk destabilizing a situation, we prefer staying with something exactly as we learned it. Step-by-step instructions and plenty of practice are very effective for preserving how-to knowledge. With abstract information, such as a philosophical idea, we seek clarification to preserve and stick with the meaning that was originally intended by those who developed or presided over the idea.

Social roles and institutions, such as the family, our community, and our national and ethnic affiliations are long-lasting and act to stabilize life as a whole. Reenacting traditions and rites, whether singing Christmas carols or celebrating birthdays or bar mitzvahs, reinforces this stabilizing effect. Since we are a part of these institutions, we have a responsibility to review and maintain standards and precedents, whether these are time-tested methodologies, the positions of authority figures who've earned respect, or carefully hammered out public policies. We fulfill jury duty summons, look both ways before crossing the street, keep tax returns seven years, and hold doors open for those who deserve it. Even in times of uncertainty we remember that change is the one constant: we are not the first generation to experience disruption or chaos, and we will be passing on the predictable standards to our descendants.

FIG. 4.1. Cognitive snapshot of introverted sensing

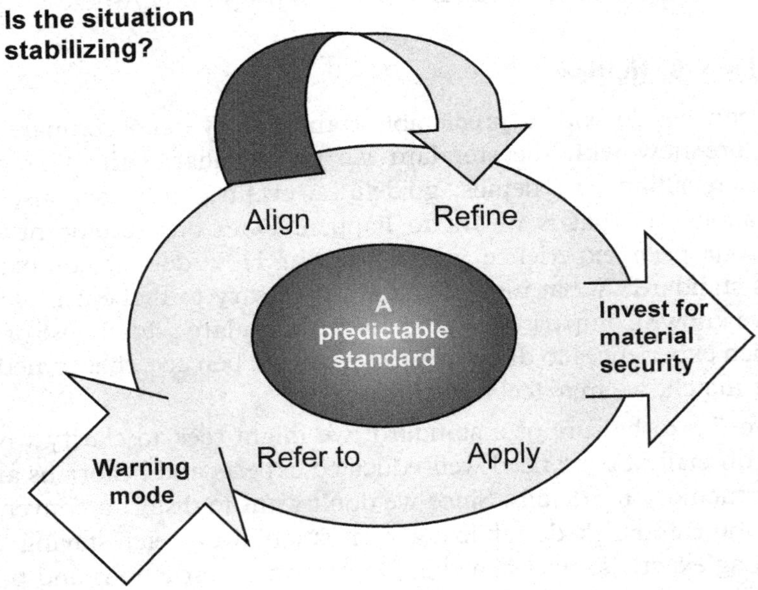

At the core of introverted Sensing is a predictable standard, such as an institution, custom, or authority. When we go into a warning mode, we compare a situation with the standard, reviewing the standard if necessary. We can refer to, align, refine, and apply a predictable standard. Applying often means investing for material security. We reflect on our predictable standard by asking, does using it stabilize the situation?

Since life can be unpredictable, a reliable guide, map, or set of sign-posts is prized. This guide might be how to succeed in college, how to raise children, or even how to die peacefully. Our elders are role models for how to handle such tasks. Similarly, we value having extra resources on hand for emergencies. And what should we hold at bay that's destabilizing? Stockpiling, planning, monitoring, and investment lead to material, social, and emotional security.

Even with change we remain solid. In new surroundings we might look around for what's familiar and hold strongly to that, perhaps applying what we know to make things more comfortable, such as ordering familiar food while traveling. We are not easily swayed by the present since it doesn't last compared to long-term institutions, commitments, and relationships. When a new standard is called for, we still can ask what precedent tells us. We build on the work of others, doing careful research and cataloging existing ideas before trying something new. We add to tradition, standing on the shoulders of those who have come before us. These precedents are not to be lightly abandoned.

People who prefer introverted Sensing draw on a storehouse of detailed standards and experiences to maintain a steady, comfortable pace as they navigate life and make sense of all aspects of living.

Mind-Set and Feedback

Using introverted Sensing requires that we maintain reliable prac-tices. This often means sustaining and stabilizing group and cul-tural institutions and giving a warning or setting up roadblocks when standards are threatened. Even if we dislike something new, if a deci-sion for change has been reached through established institutions and civic values, then we can accept it. If we didn't, we would be a disruptive element. Change is acceptable so long as it is carefully monitored and managed.

We know a standard is reliable if it stabilizes a situation. When a customary way of doing things is stable in the midst of great change, we find a tremendous feeling of comfort and relief.

Possible Misuses

Sometimes use of the introverted Sensing process becomes rigid and dominating because of stress or because it is used without skill and without other processes to balance it. When this occurs, we may

- Find ourselves engaging in pack-rat behavior, hoarding material goods to feel secure
- React more intensely than we want to when we recall memories of a negative experience, as if the experience is happening again
- Hear from others that we are overly focused on warnings about safety and lack and comfort
- Be perceived by others as somewhat stuck in the past or rigidly adhering to a known standard
- Find it hard to keep up with changes; for example, when our bank changes its customary, familiar procedures

Case Studies

The following vignettes illustrate introverted Sensing. The first is an everyday personal situation and the second is an organizational situation that includes other processes.

Case A

Heather is out touring in an unfamiliar foreign city. The ancient ruins she and her friends saw earlier were very interesting because they reminded her that however much things seem to change, daily human activities like going to the market, raising children, and attending religious services haven't changed at all. The tour guide was extremely detailed and clear. As Heather listened, the guide impressed upon her what life was like in ancient times. But right  now, she's separated from her friends and feels disoriented. The sun peeks out and she reorients herself to go north back to the hotel. Her cell phone rings. It's a friend. His voice is reassuring. She passes by a flower shop and notices a fine rare species that she remembers from her childhood. She feels comforted by this familiar sight, realizing that even in such a faraway city she can find commonalities with her own life.

Case B

Jocelyn is the most reliable diplomat the corps has. She was trained by some of the most skillful members of the older generation and soaked up everything, educating herself beyond the courses and fieldwork. The world is in constant flux, yet Jocelyn knows that from history we can understand what might occur. Many parties she meets come from highly unstable places. As she meets them she draws on her storehouse of past experiences—the patterns of problems and specific solutions that have  worked. She draws from these to suggest positive possibilities. Often the places need stabilizing before she can try to establish a major institutional change, but these parties also need hope. A few light touches of humor help too. Jocelyn reads a great deal of history. She has a deep sense that one can rely on civilization.

Perspective Shifting

Here are some suggestions for how to communicate with, learn from, and influence someone who is using introverted Sensing.

- **Communicating to Build Rapport**
  - Ask what predictable standard the other person is using. He or she may refer to a manual, established procedure, leader, parent, authoritative or influential figure, historical precedent, institution, law, value, tradition, meme, or custom. Use the other person's terms when you converse.
  - To gauge how the person feels about adhering to the standard, ask if he or she feels secure or is feeling uncomfortable about an unstable situation. Use inclusive language, such as "our standard" as opposed to "your standard."

- **Learning to Build New Skills**
  - Find out about the standard. Educate yourself on who established it and when. Was there a different standard before then? What promoted the need for the standard? Who maintains it now, and what kind of training was required? This may take quite a bit of research.

- Ask the other person to describe how using the standard has a stabilizing effect on a situation. At what point is extra vigilance needed, and what signs indicate that the stabilizing effect is working? For example, how and when do we cross from free speech to inciting problems? Most likely you will discover there are ever-more detailed standards to review and learn about.

- **Influencing for Best Use**
  - Consider whether other standards are being compromised or sacrificed in the service of the current one.
  - Ask how much the person has been able to go into a warning mode and what predictable standards he or she might have forgotten about or probably needs to review again.

- **Helping to Discover New Outcomes**
  - Ask the other person whether the situation is being stabilized as much as it can. That is, has following this standard really protected our values? You may need to give examples of past situations where another standard worked better.
  - If the person is dissatisfied, could another predictable standard also provide stability? (The person may not know what that new standard might be.)

There is always a comparison to be made,
and if it is familiar, it is to be trusted.

Developing Introverted Sensing

The following exercises will help you develop the introverted Sensing process. Get your self-assessment score from the beginning of this chapter and then set your starting point using the chart below.

If you scored	Then start with
0–3	The Introductory Exercises
4–9	The Basic Exercises
10+	The Advanced Exercises

As you work through the coming exercises, you may find some are particularly challenging. Include all the following steps to get more satisfying use of this process:

1. To access the process in the most effective way, go into a protective and concerned warning mode. (See pages 166–167 to enter this mode.)

2. Access the core of the process: which predictable standard is appropriate to stabilize the situation?

3. Engage in best-use activities, such as comparing the situation with what you are familiar with or reviewing your storehouse of experiences for what to expect.

4. Try for a desired outcome by investing (time, money, etc.) toward ensuring future security.

5. Get feedback and calibrate: is the standard we're relying on providing a sense of security?

6. Integrate your use of introverted Sensing with other cognitive processes (usually extraverted Thinking or extraverted Feeling).

As you develop this process, you'll be able to engage these steps all at once for increasingly coordinated and smooth use.

Introductory Exercises

These exercises will help you get comfortable researching details, finding what is predictable, and becoming more familiar with your background.

INTERVIEW AN ELDER

Sit down and interview one of the oldest people you know, preferably someone who knows your family's or organization's past very well and ideally someone you share roots with. Give the person time to speak, and be ready to hear information you didn't know or plan on asking about. Ask questions to get details and clarity on what happened when, with whom, where, and so on.

RESEARCH ALL THE DETAILS

Pick elements from the interview to research, ideally areas that relate further to you and also to a larger historical picture. You might research a foreign country or faraway town that your ancestors came from or a prestigious role someone played, such as being the head chef to a king. Research as much as you can. Read books and watch factual films. Go to a large library and sift through relevant newspaper and magazine articles. Understand the context as well as the specifics. For the king's chef, what was going on in the country at that time? Visit other people to find out more. And look through old letters, heirlooms, and other items of the period.

CONTINUE A TRADITION

Reflect on what you've unearthed. What feels as though it really reconnects you to your roots? Add an element of that tradition to your life, whether it's a restored photo, a recipe, or a piece of artwork an ancestor created.

Basic Exercises

These exercises will help you get comfortable exploring predictable standards, from world and family history and traditions to how your organization and community work.

READ A LOT OF HISTORY

Pick some reputable books—ones that are factual, are written by long-time experts, and give a window into daily life as well as big events. Consider books that were published fifty years or more ago, if possible, in addition to recent books to get a more thorough perspective. As you read, consider which institutions, organizations, movements, and ideas have lasted. How did they respond to challenge and change in order to survive and thrive? What conventions have changed or remained? And what are some lessons for today? Try to step back to see the present as a moment in the panoramic sweep of human history and human nature. Similarly, look at institutions, organizations, and ideas that have mostly vanished. Why did they fail? You will likely find failures in character, lack of preparation for adversity, and the inability to uphold key values. In a vanished organization you might uncover failures in service, production quality, and adherence to a mission.

As you read, focus on comparisons with today, observing how life or standards differ. The Roman Empire and the American Revolution can be as relevant, if not more so, than last year's brightest stars in the news. A family-run organization that's lasted two hundred years is certainly impressive. Focus on what made these civilizations, organizations, movements, and ideas enduring and successful. Focus on details and character.

READ BIOGRAPHIES

Soak up information about the lives that have influenced the world today, for good or ill, as well as the lives of people who are role models for success. What were their family lives and career lives like? Pay special attention to qualities of character that these people held or developed as they weathered adversities. What were their beliefs and the ideas they followed? Who were their role models? As you read, compare these notable individuals and groups to people you know now in similar positions and to yourself.

RESEARCH THE HISTORY OF AN IDEA

Ideas powerfully shape our lives. They affect how we think and the decisions we make. Choose an idea related to your career or in a field of high interest to you. As ideas are handed down and passed around, especially by nonexperts or through questionable sources like the Internet, they tend to get distorted and lose their original meaning and depth. Therefore, as you research, learn not only about the original thinkers and their intended meanings but also how, when, and by whom the idea has been carried and distorted. Document everything you read and the people you interview, and then write a report or lecture on what you've learned. Include references for others to confirm your research and build on what you've done.

LEARN HOW YOUR ORGANIZATION WORKS

Focus on an institution relevant to your daily life, such as the organization you work for or encounter the most, perhaps your local government, which often has tremendous influence on the quality of life. Get to know this organization or institution in detail. What are its responsibilities? What roles or positions exist and who currently fills these roles? If you work in a big company, do you know the president's name? If you are part of a far-flung network of researchers, do you know the names and writings of the lead experts? Consider how you can use this information to solve problems—whom do you need to go to and what questions do you need to ask? Similarly, note whom to pay attention to because one day you might fill one of these higher roles. Knowing an organization also allows you to help and direct others.

REVIEW YOUR ORGANIZATION'S HISTORY AND STANDARDS

Who was the founder of your organization? Even large, impersonal organizations have traditions started by their founders; many times these traditions are known by only a few people. What ups and downs has the organization faced over time? What standards or procedures exist as a result of this history to make the organization what it is today?

CARRY ON TRADITIONS

Learn in depth about your family traditions and ethnic background, everything from food and clothing to religion and mythology. This may take some time, perhaps many years. Don't rush it. Simply continue over time to steadily learn and absorb these details while incorporating them into your life. Carry on in your own life, and the lives of your family and community, as many traditions as possible. Over time you might learn your ancestors' language, which might just be Old English. Also visit your family's place of origin. Honor and sustain your background by cooking traditional meals, going to community festivals, and so on. Consider how your background informs who you are as a person.

CULTIVATE GOOD HABITS

Good habits sustain us when circumstances are grim and open doors to better opportunities. These include grooming and etiquette, proper spelling and pronunciation, and thorough knowledge of social and cultural conventions. Practice expanding your vocabulary. Dress in a way that is comfortable and familiar to the people around you.

FIND AND STAY IN YOUR COMFORT ZONE

In any situation, find the places, people to talk to, and ways of doing things that are most comfortable and familiar to you. These might include foods, music, and other details. As the environment changes, or as you go somewhere else, move without hurrying and stay with what's comfortable. Where you are most comfortable is a good starting point to try new things, and a good place to return in order to relax. Also, share with others what makes you comfortable and uncomfortable. This sharing can create a sense of community when everyone knows and attends to where his or her comfort zone is.

Advanced Exercises

These exercises will help you hone your basic use of the introverted Sensing process and develop some advanced use. Learn to take a more active role in maintaining and passing on what's reliable.

IDENTIFY WHAT'S UNSAFE OR INSECURE

Look around your organization, community, culture, or family environment and compare what you see with what you've now learned are predictable standards. Look for what is unsafe, in violation of established values, problematic, or otherwise suggestive of a possible future turn for the worse. This might be something as seemingly minor as a dangerous parking lot or as scandalous as a prominent leader not properly fulfilling the responsibilities of his or her position. Look for people acting out of a desire for personal gain, people who lack competence and training, or people who are poor judges or poor examples of good character.

STABILIZE THE PRESENT

After researching your history, culture, organization, and other institutions and learning how people have handled problems in the past, you are in a solid position to help stabilize and correct problem areas right now. Find out what resources are available to help you resolve the problem. These resources might be supervisory committees, ethics panels, an ombudsman, or a particular procedure. Go through these channels so you aren't perceived as a problem. The result might be a change in standards, a safety mechanism, or a required certification process. Going through proper channels may take some time, particularly in large or far-flung organizations where there are many people to consult and procedures or standards to review before moving ahead. Remember that your organization is itself a standard. You are helping to maintain the reliability and prestige of this standard.

VOLUNTEER TO HELP

Sometimes no existing standard covers a particular concern or dangerous situation, or no one is competent or willing to apply the existing standards. It may be that no one is looking out to stabilize a situation and shepherd the people in it at all. Now is the time for you to volunteer if you feel sufficiently comfortable and ready to do so. Having others at your side to assist and advise you can make this step more comfortable. Consider the appropriate way to volunteer. It might be to fill a support or research position, assist other members of your organization, work with your peers toward a common end, or even go outside the organization to give or get help. In a broader way, volunteering might mean running for public office or performing in some other major position of responsibility. Volunteer roles, filled responsibly, often lead to official positions later.

ESTABLISH NEW PREDICTABLE STANDARDS

As times change and we face new challenges, new standards are needed to sustain the growth process. An example is an individual's journey through the important points of life, such as going to college, getting a job, getting married, and having children. At each of these points, we benefit when we can turn to reliable sources of information and guidance. When helping others, you can draw upon your own rich storehouse of personal experience and upon the knowledge you have soaked up of others' experiences to give advice. As you establish the new standard, get feedback so you can be sure it is accepted and carried out. Also make sure that the standard maintains the quality or value of what has come before, whether it is an organization's good name, people's reputations, the value of an idea, or confidence in a particular brand.

ANTICIPATE THE FUTURE

What do you expect to happen in the future? You can form expectations by looking at the paths society has laid out and the experience of those who've come before you and even by consulting experts who are known for predicting from trends. When you were in high school you probably had a good idea what was coming next—either college or a job. Most people expect to get married—marriage being an institution older than history. We all grow old and can expect to need support when we decline.

INVEST FOR THE FUTURE

Investing for the future includes saving, storing, and planning, as well as monitoring and protecting what has been set aside for the future. Investment might mean money and material goods, but it also means investing in a stable, productive, and successful life. Getting a solid education helps ensure a higher-paying job than you can expect with a lack of education. Investing a summer in learning etiquette can open doors throughout your life, as can learning how to balance your checkbook. Also, have a backup plan or safety net. Communities and organizations provide safety nets, and being a responsible member of your community brings respect, which can mean care and support in your old age.

WORK AT A STEADY, EVEN PACE

With so many details to manage, with so much accumulation of knowledge, and with the high pace of change, it is worthwhile to work at a steady, even pace each day as an investment in your health and to accomplish as much as possible. Find a place to live and stay where the people and practices are familiar and comforting.

SHEPHERD AND SUSTAIN THE NEXT GENERATION
We are neither the first nor likely the last generation. Take everything that you've learned and use it to contribute to and maintain a safe, stable environment for your children and the next generation, passing on your knowledge and experience. This means participating in your family life, your community, and your nation.

5

Exploring the
Emerging Patterns

Understanding and Developing Extraverted Intuiting

Benefits for Self-Leadership

As you develop extraverted Intuiting, you will
- Be more imaginative when problem solving
- Have greater awareness of interpersonal dynamics and people's behavioral patterns
- Feel excited to pursue novelty and change
- Enjoy more of life's humorous moments

Assessing Current Development

Before continuing, check the phrases in the table that describe you well.

Part 1
☐ Often perceive how a pattern or dynamic is emerging.
☐ Offer various unrelated ideas and see what potential they might suggest.
☐ Keep following tangents and new ideas without limiting yourself to one.
Part 2
☐ Engage life's magical moments and coincidences as they happen.
☐ Engage in brainstorming and trust what emerges from it.
Part 3
☐ Try new ideas and interactions because they are new and different.
☐ Enjoy playing with random interconnections and patterns.
☐ Weave into the current dynamics of a situation aspects of other, random-seeming contexts.

Scoring: Assign one point to items in part 1, two points to items in part 2, and three points to items in part 3.

Total points: 12

A score above nine indicates a likely preference for extraverted Intuiting. A score from four to nine indicates a possible supporting preference or development from life experience. A score below four suggests a lack of development.

Understanding How Extraverted Intuiting Works

At the core of extraverted Intuiting is an <u>emergent pattern.</u> A pattern is a set of relationships. Perhaps a nanny is to a troubled household and its parents as a consultant is to a troubled company and its executives? Or not. Emergence means this idea may lead to more and better ideas. Patterns emerge from interactions and interrelationships between people and ideas, objects and emotions, paupers and princesses. We notice and follow these patterns as they keep surfacing, trusting they lead somewhere interesting. In the briefest moment, two or more threads of meaning may converge and suggest a possibility awaiting further exploration.

Best-Use Activities

What can we do with an emergent pattern? We might explore what we are perceiving to better understand it. This often involves thinking of another similar situation, then testing to see if the pattern still holds. Perhaps we are noticing a dynamic between three friends: two of them get along well until the third arrives. We consider another set of friends and see whether we perceive the same dynamic among them. If so, perhaps we borrow and interject some of what we've learned from that other relationship into the current one to see what happens.

We might mention the patterns and dynamics we perceive as they're happening. In a typical conversation with a friend we ask, "How's it going?" Later, as a conversation grows stale, we might say, "So how about this conversation, how's it going?" Consider what you are wondering about as you read this paragraph. We keep splitting off from what's happening now to explore what could be.

As something stimulates our minds, we can juggle many tangents at once without limiting our thoughts to one idea. If we are composing a story or a business market strategy we might brainstorm numerous intriguing possibilities. Some of them might not sound practical or relevant, but considering them jumpstarts our imagination. What if we wrote the story scene so that multiple meanings collide? What if we weave together marketing strategies? We can combine multiple patterns at once to discover even more new possibilities or we may find ourselves suddenly speculating with many questions. What if we explore a new market? Possibilities and connections can arise as a flood, fast paced and seemingly chaotic, yet some people can instantly pick out the most humorous, effective, or insightful possibility. What's exciting about brainstorming is when we trust the emergent process to get something better. We keep asking, what if? And what else is possible? We float various unrelated ideas just to see where they might lead.

With each idea we get, we might offer inferences and hypotheses. Perhaps we wonder how a meaningful coincidence might continue evolving along a particular trajectory. Perhaps the chance arrival of an old friend

FIG. 5.1. Cognitive snapshot of extraverted intuiting

Is this hypothesis meaningful?

Align   Refine

An emergent pattern

Shift a situation's dynamics

Inference mode   Refer to   Apply

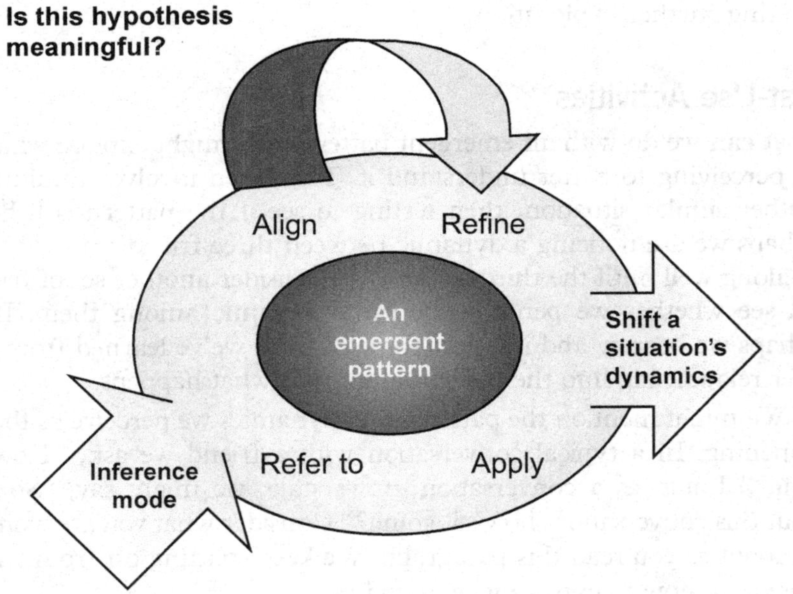

At the core of extraverted Intuiting is an emergent pattern, such as a dynamic among individuals in a group. When we go into an inference mode, we wonder how this pattern fits across various contexts, generating hypotheses. We can refer to, align, refine, and apply an emergent pattern. Applying often means shifting a situation's dynamics. We reflect on the emergent pattern by asking, is it meaningful?

may afford a new business venture or may inform us of a new option. Or we might wonder, what if a pattern didn't exist? What if we had never known this friend? Often just considering the idea is enough, and we don't feel a need to act on it, evaluate it, define it, or structure it. Doing so would foreclose further thinking. Similarly, seeing something through to its end or addressing details may become boring. The idea of something novel is tantalizing and exciting. We might share our hypotheses, promote them, make fun of them, or pocket them for a rainy day.

We can play along with a pattern, act to shift a pattern so events flow in a new way, or interrupt it with something unrelated. Perhaps after seeing our three friends' dynamic one too many times we notice a moment in which we can intervene and catalyze a change. We weave into the situation aspects of another relationship. The way the situation changes may lead to a new story, particularly if others join us extemporaneously. When the interrelationships are hidden to others, it's as if an invisible hand is guiding the situation or a magic spell has been cast over it. Imaginatively playing with scenarios and combining possibilities in this way is fun in and of itself.

People who prefer extraverted Intuiting rely on their abstract perceptiveness, openness to potential, and quick imagination to navigate life and make sense of all aspects of living.

Mind-Set and Feedback

Using extraverted Intuiting requires that we remain highly attentive to interactions in the moment while also being split off from a situation and its details. We remain open to following any number of possibilities at once as they arise, without settling on one. Everything and anything is fodder for the mind attuned to noticing patterns. The patterns that emerge can bring tremendous meaning and novelty.

All the patterns have a pattern; that too emerges. Among many possible patterns one often stands out, suggesting the greatest potential. When we perceive this great potential we feel excited and creative.

Possible Misuses

Sometimes use of the extraverted Intuiting process becomes rigid and dominating because of stress or because it is used without skill and without other processes to balance it. When this occurs, we may

- Engage in magical thinking, interpreting a coincidence as more significant than it probably is

- Overgeneralize and assume we understand something just because we've hypothesized about it
- Use humor when we're uncomfortable and find it hard to engage in serious discussion
- Imagine seeing or hearing things that aren't there—imagination impinges on our sense of what's real
- Misinterpret the intended meaning of someone's actions, so the person feels we're misreading between the lines

Case Studies

The following vignettes illustrate extraverted Intuiting. The first is an everyday situation and the second illustrates use with other processes in an organizational setting.

Case A

As Carrie moved into her first apartment, she wondered how people become neighbors. Why do certain folks come together and not others, and whom might she meet? Patterns instantly came to her awareness: distance between apartments, times that people come and go, and possible jobs, incomes, and leisure activities. She compared her thoughts to a mental picture of college life—a close match of patterns. Volunteer dorm advisors bring people together to relax; Carrie wondered, maybe that's what this place needs. She kept exploring the idea over the next few days. Students share a process—starting the school year, midterms, winter and spring breaks—yet everyone is out of phase with each other. After chatting with some interesting neighbors, she put up fliers for a get-together, offering "Come take a vacation from life." Let's just see what happens, she thought.

Case B

Eric is a public advocate, often working with elected officials to find and try new approaches to problems. He's great working with a diverse group of people and gets excited as everyone plays off each other and people generate creative strategies together. He's aware of the many interrelationships and dynamics in a problem, the people involved, and their dynamics—and at every moment his mind is playing out scenarios and offering up ideas. How can we do this? How will the public respond if we do that? He plays devil's advocate with others just as well. After many years, he can draw upon a rich storehouse of past experiences for inspiration, and colleagues admire how often his suggestions work well. He hopes that someday one of his really big ideas will get enough support to emerge as a new standard.

Perspective Shifting

Here are some suggestions for how to communicate with, learn from, and influence someone who is using extraverted Intuiting.

- **Communicating to Build Rapport**
  - Ask what patterns the other person notices. The person may refer to a dynamic, interrelationship, meaning, hypothesis, thread, possibility, story, strategy, moment, inference, or analysis or use another abstract term. Use this person's term when you converse.
  - To gauge how the person feels about the emergent pattern, reflect back to the person the emotion you detect—excitement, inspiration, creativity, passion, or involvement or if he or she feels bored and finds the situation flat, empty, superficial, stifling, or uninspiring.

- **Learning to Build New Skills**
  - Ask about the emergent pattern. What elements—people, companies, and so on—are part of the pattern? Ask the person to describe dynamics he or she notices among the elements. Together, explore other contexts that show similar patterns.
  - Ask the person to describe possible intervention points. What might someone say or do to shift the pattern? Don't push for action; the person will be more open to hypothetical suggestions. Ask this person to describe two or more cues that tell him or her a dynamic is forming or is about to dissipate. What signals to this person that it's time to leave a situation?

- **Influencing for Best Use**
  - Where is the emerging pattern going? Ask the person about dynamics he or she doesn't quite understand yet. Also, who is affected by the pattern and how?
  - Ask how much the person has been able to go into an inference mode where he or she experiences sudden episodes of brainstorming, magical moments, or creative flow. How often has this person been able to check out hypotheses and inferences?

- **Helping to Discover New Outcomes**
  - Ask the other person whether the emergent pattern is as all-encompassing as it could be. That is, does the "best fit" pattern really capture the situation? You may need to give examples of alternate hypotheses.
  - If the person is dissatisfied, is a totally different pattern waiting to be discovered that better explains the situation? (The person may not know what that new pattern might be.)

There are always other potential perspectives
and new meanings to discover.

Developing Extraverted Intuiting

The following exercises will help you develop the extraverted Intuiting process. Get your self-assessment score from the beginning of this chapter and then set your starting point using the chart below.

If you scored	Then start with
0–3	The Introductory Exercises
4–9	The Basic Exercises
10+	The Advanced Exercises

As you work through the coming exercises, you may find some are particularly challenging. Include all the following steps to get more satisfying use of this process:

1. To access the process in the most effective way, go into a perceptive inference mode. (See pages 166–167 to enter this mode.)

2. Access the core of the process: identify the emerging pattern of relationships or dynamics.

3. Engage in best-use activities, such as imagining alternate scenarios to see if the pattern holds or noticing how the dynamics continue to evolve or shift.

4. Try for a desired outcome by intervening to shift the dynamics, often by bringing in something that is out of context.

5. Get feedback and calibrate: which pattern of interrelationships is the strongest or the best fit?

6. Integrate your use of extraverted Intuiting with other cognitive processes (usually introverted Thinking or introverted Feeling).

As you develop this process, you'll be able to engage these steps all at once for increasingly coordinated and smooth use.

Introductory Exercises

These exercises will help you get comfortable imaginatively drawing on other contexts to enrich your perception of interactions going on around you.

NOTICE A PATTERN

Observe your environment and consider how two objects might be related. You might notice how a penny and a quarter have different qualities. A quarter is bigger and worth more, while the penny is smaller and worth so little that many people often give or throw them away. Brainstorm as many ways as possible for how they compare to each other. The result is a pattern of differences.

LINK THE PATTERN TO OTHER SITUATIONS

What else has this pattern of differences? We might think about advice. Advice that we pay for and comes with prestige (perceived as "bigger" and worth more) may be more likely to be taken seriously than free advice that we receive from a random acquaintance (perceived as "smaller" and worth less). We don't know whether this is the case; it's a hypothesis. We have mapped one set of relationships onto another. Now brainstorm other contexts. Perhaps in times of emergency, rescuers are more likely to rush aid and support to a place with large numbers of people who are wealthier than to a location with few people who are poorer. And perhaps you recently sided with one friend against another in a dispute: maybe you were following this pattern. You can probably think of many patterns like this.

KEEP ASKING WHAT-IFS

Now ask as many what-if questions as possible. What if you added a third type of coin? What about someone who eschews money? Would these changes reflect a variation on the pattern, perhaps in how people might advise or rescue? There are no set answers yet, only more questions.

Basic Exercises

These exercises will help you get comfortable responding to patterns and dynamics as they emerge, from shifting perspective to acting on meaningful convergences.

REINTERPRET POSSIBLE MEANINGS

Consider what each situation would be like if the perceived pattern was reversed or went away. For example, discrimination was once accepted, but today human lives are officially given equal value. How might we reinterpret the penny-quarter relationship? The penny is made of copper and the quarter is made of aluminum. The quarter isn't materially worth more than the penny, though it is officially granted greater worth. Even their material worth as metals is determined by use and marketing and lacks any absolute value.

LOCATE OTHER CONTEXTS IN THE PRESENT

Imagine various situations you know and note which ones appear in the current context. Remember junior high school? What interactions or dynamics were typical? Now overlay these interactions or dynamics on your current situation and identify similarities and differences. How is your context the "same old story" and what is new?

SHIFT PERSPECTIVES

Imagine your current situation from alternate perspectives. You may be crossing the street, but what if you were one of the people in a car turning left or in a waiting car or in the red-and-black car over there (find it in your imagination)? What if you were another pedestrian crossing the same street? Imagine what each person's life might be like to understand the overall situation more fully. If you engage your imagination this way, then you may be more skillful in relating the situation to others when describing it to them later. The more perspectives you include, the more likely it is that the story you describe will be understood by those listening.

NOTICE MOMENTS OF CONVERGENCE

Convergence means two or more things—objects, people, ideas—coming together. A convergence might be a surprise, or it might be expected if we are usually attuned to what's going on around us. If we bring people of different disciplines to a conference or a project, a convergence of ideas may result. Or the convergence might be serendipitous—a meaningful coincidence. You might randomly run into an old friend who just learned this morning about a job offer that happens to suit you perfectly, just when you were experiencing dissatisfaction with your current job.

ACT ON MEANINGFUL CONVERGENCES

Highly meaningful convergences can be very rare, perhaps occurring once in a lifetime. Perhaps we're flipping through television channels with a close friend at our side and we stumble upon a show that influences the friend to discuss the possibility of taking the relationship into romance. If we had been alone or hadn't turned to that channel, then this talk would have happened later or perhaps never. These moments allow unique conversations or interactions to occur. They are rare because they bring together elements that don't normally meet. Acting on these convergences—opening them up and exploring them—can change our lives and those around us.

FILL YOUR ENVIRONMENT WITH MULTIPLE INPUTS

Turn on the television and the radio, open a book, surf the Web, talk on the phone, and look out the window. These multiple sources of input increase the potential for meaningful convergence. They also place side by side various patterns for our consideration. And they drown out the present context, which can limit us to one way of perceiving or being in the world.

TRY NEW IDEAS

New ideas include new technology, new methods, newly emerging trends, new writing and music, new planets, new anything. Being an "early adopter" allows us to experience and explore unknown territories. Install a new operating system on your computer. Buy a book by a brand-new author. Explore a prototype of a new musical instrument. Travel to a country no one you know has ever been to before. Interview people about the latest craze or trend. Try everything that intrigues you and explore the potential of each.

EXPLORE POTENTIAL IDEAS

Brainstorm a variety of what-if scenarios and potential implications. What if people could implant a device in their children's bodies to track them? What if everyone could work at home? What if we developed technology to read animals' minds? With each question, consider how society would react. How would the children react? Would a classic dynamic emerge, such as "build a better mousetrap and you will get a smarter mouse"? Would the patterns in society remarkably shift in some way? Explore each idea from all angles, considering all the patterns you are aware of. Then brainstorm ways to communicate these patterns in ways people can understand now, as if you were marketing or promoting the new idea.

Advanced Exercises

These exercises will help you hone your basic use of the extraverted Intuiting process and develop some advanced use. Learn to take a more active role in shaping situations and shifting interactions.

TRAVEL TO NEW CULTURES

Culture is a powerful blinder—for all the interactions, stories, and possibilities we may perceive, we could be aware of many more if only we had grown up in another culture or, perhaps better yet, in multiple cultures. Travel allows us to experience other cultures and thus, like an anthropologist, resee our own culture as well as see emergent patterns across cultures. Travel also provokes the imagination, and the convergence of reality and the imagined is itself a further source of new ideas and potential.

TRAVEL TO FICTIONAL WORLDS

Explore new worlds through books, films, plays, interactive art, or even virtual worlds. Many of these imaginary worlds may be less rich or more "programmed" than real ones, but some can be entertaining enough as you try to figure out the patterns at play. Some fiction truly takes advantage of the medium to combine contexts we don't see together in the real world, whether these are strip mall vampires or talking pigs in outer space. Consider that just being a part of reality means losing potential possibilities.

EXPLORE ORDINARY SITUATIONS

Consider everyday activities, such as going to the market. We engage in these activities so often, do we really see them anymore? What happens in these situations? Explore and take in the dynamics, stories, and interaction patterns. Link these to other situations, real and imagined. You might interview people and get a look behind the scenes. What happens when special situations arise? Do all the workers in the dairy section drink milk? Similarly, how about the people around us who aren't "seeing" the market? The moment people ignore their environment, do they forget to act in expected ways and act more like themselves? After exploring, you may never see these everyday activities in the same way again.

KEEP EXPLORING DIFFERENT CONTEXTS

Life is brimming with various worlds to explore—the theater, sports, museums, nature, urban and rural life, academia, the military, religion, and spirituality. Go to a place and observe or interact to discover the patterns and interconnections within the context. Consider not only what's in each context but also places and times where they intersect—such as religion in the military or the representation of sports in music. Also explore the implied links between each. Keep exploring, not dwelling too long in one place.

FOCUS ON DYNAMICS

Consider interactions that change over time or occur in a pattern. A married couple, or a boss and an employee, might interact in predictable ways. Observe what happens just before a dynamic becomes visible to all. Notice what's happening around the people, not just the two of them. What happens just before an argument, for example? What communication signals are traded? What body postures or words do people use? Collect these observations and compare them to the observed dynamics in other situations.

HIGHLIGHT A PATTERN OR DYNAMIC FOR OTHERS TO SEE

Connect and intermix two aspects of your life—take an element from one context and swap it with an element from a parallel context. Such a swap can highlight a particular argument or unique meaning or evoke humor in difficult situations. A variation on this is to say something plausible for the situation but that is not actually true. First, consider other situations with the pattern you perceive now but with differing details. Then highlight the pattern and insert the desired details. You might also write a story this way.

DETECT OUT-OF-PATTERN BEHAVIOR

Explore when someone or something does not fit an otherwise cohesive pattern in a situation. Maybe something is wrong or something is not what it appears to be. Also consider that if you have the option to interact in an atypical way, then others do too. Out-of-pattern behavior can also indicate an impending convergence.

INFER POSSIBLE TACIT INFORMATION

Many times, information is not well advertised. For example, someone might be feeling unwell, worrying about a situation, or feeling stressed but not say anything or show any visible signs of distress. If you suspect something, refer to the overall pattern of interactions, considering similar situations and exploring what was present in those situations.

BORROW A PATTERN

Consider how some teen actors can convincingly play their grandparents or act out situations they've never experienced. Observe the interrelationships of someone's life and then "wear" those as your own. Join a community theater group or write a story, trying on the life of someone else. You can weave a metaphorical story mirroring a current situation and then retell the story in a humorous way to help others see the pattern without having to face the actual situation. This can be particularly helpful when someone comes to you with a problem and wonders what to do. Observing your own stories makes it easier to free yourself to live others' stories.

TRANSITION TO A NEW PATTERN

Help someone transition away from unhealthy patterns by matching yourself to the current pattern and then slowly introducing elements of a related, healthier pattern. You can do this by joining a person or group in that person's or group's behavior and then engaging in a bridging behavior that helps the person or group be more open to a new behavior that otherwise wouldn't fit what's going on.

EXPLORE THE LANDSCAPE OF PATTERNS

Look for a metapattern. Underlying all the interrelationships of life
are a few patterns, or perhaps even one. Just as you have explored the
dynamics between people, objects, and actions in and across situations,
explore the interrelationships between patterns. You may discover a
hidden system at play.

6

Transforming with a Metaperspective

Understanding and Developing Introverted Intuiting

Benefits for Self-Leadership

As you develop introverted Intuiting, you will
- Envision an energizing future
- Have greater awareness of your own and others' inner potential
- Come up with innovative ideas that no one has thought of before
- Transform how you think about life

Assessing Current Development

Before continuing, check the phrases in the table that describe you well.

Part 1
☐ Experience a sudden "aha" realization about a problem, coming as if out of nowhere.
☐ Feel attracted to the symbolic, archetypal, or mysterious.
☐ Experience a premonition or foresee the unexpected.
Part 2
☐ Gain a profound realization from a mystical state or catharsis.
☐ Push your mind to envision a solution to a problem that hasn't come up yet.
Part 3
☐ Synthesize a new idea that transcends various opposing points of view.
☐ Achieve a metamorphosis, definitive insight, or powerful vision of change.
☐ Transform yourself in a specific way by focusing inward on a way you foresee you'll need to be in the future.

Scoring: Assign one point to items in part 1, two points to items in part 2, and three points to items in part 3.

Total points: 8

A score above nine indicates a likely preference for introverted Intuiting. A score from four to nine indicates a possible supporting preference or development from life experience. A score below four suggests a lack of development.

Understanding How Introverted Intuiting Works

At the core of introverted Intuiting is a metaperspective—the highest level or the most flexible frame of mind or form of behavior that each of us currently has access to. One metaperspective is our own mind's workings: we can shut out the world, quiet our minds, and ask our unconscious to take us to a new level of awareness. Every perspective has its purpose and power. With understanding we can shift between perspectives at will, each one giving us insights and energizing us with a different "way to be" to solve otherwise intractable problems or to accomplish a vision of the future. We often evoke our perspectives by focusing on symbols, archetypes, totems, and other abstractions, such as visual models.

Best-Use Activities

What can we do from a metaperspective? When we disagree with someone, taking a more inclusive view reframes the debate as we notice how our perspective is one of many. The result is common ground if the other person can join us in this greater metaperspective. Similarly, we can bypass a problem by changing our thinking about it. We might ask which career path to take if we have many interests until we realize we can focus on a different question, such as what lifestyle to pursue, which might offer a single answer. If we can't comprehend something from the viewpoints we know, we might ask ourselves what we don't see.

A very powerful metaperspective is the working of our own minds. When we quiet our minds and tap into the wisdom of the unconscious, the result is an aha moment or realization. Our minds appear to function as a whole in certain hypnotic or trancelike states. When we gain access to the mind as a resource, we can access and enter these states at will. The result is a wellspring of originality, innovation, and transformation. The mind is unique in that it is teleological. This means we can orient ourselves around a future and work toward specific outcomes. This differs from natural phenomena, such as climate, where interactions promote the emergence of patterns but not toward preconceived ends. When we assume this forward-looking quality, we visualize the future and focus our energy and behavior to achieve prolific goals and tap into deep truths.

We can use this process in many ways. We might focus on a question before bed to receive insight by the morning or write a novel to focus ourselves and grow concerning a specific issue. We might do repetitive exercise or concentrate on a mandala. We might conjure up a fictional or real person in our mind and engage in an inner dialog with that person. An insight may come in a millisecond or a year and in one of many forms: through a symbol or a dream, as a sudden realization or an aha moment, or in a vision of the future or a premonition. We might experience a sudden expansion of awareness that includes the previously unthought-of,

FIG. 6.1. Cognitive snapshot of introverted intuiting

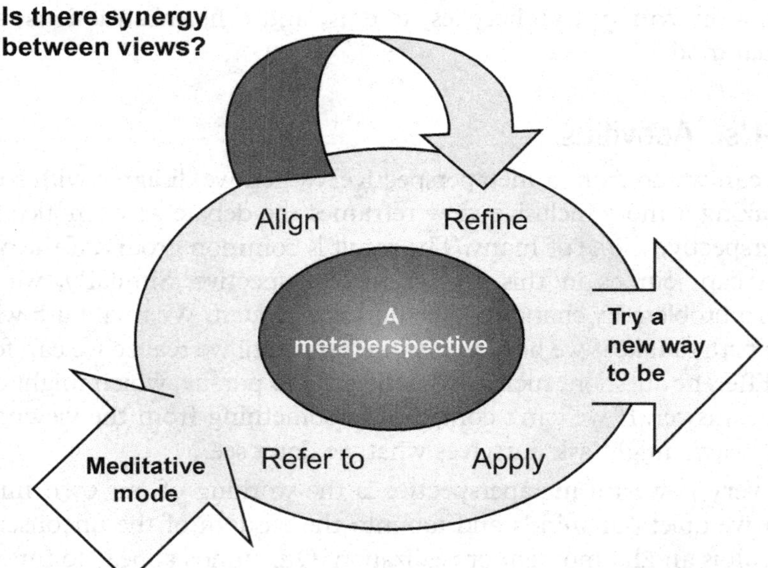

At the core of introverted Intuiting is a metaperspective—a way of seeing things that transcends competing views. When we go into a trancelike meditative mode, we withdraw from the world to get an insight or realization. We can refer to, align, refine, and apply a meta-perspective. Applying often means transformation—trying out a new way to be or a new way to think. We reflect on our metaperspective by asking, is there synergy?

perhaps a solution to a technical or personal problem we haven't even encountered yet. These realizations can be predictive, though they are not always. We might get one only when we've completely given up.

The most powerful metaperspectives result in a transformation, synthesis, or paradigm shift. All that was confusing or waiting on the edge of our mind is now accessible from a single vantage point. We can become a completely different person for a time to achieve what we are otherwise unable to do. Even then, there is still a sense of paradox, that something can and cannot be at the same time. And there remains a feeling that everything we think we know and everything we do reflect just one understanding among infinite levels of reality.

People who prefer introverted Intuiting look inward for a steady stream of realizations and mind shifting to navigate life and make sense of all aspects of living.

Mind-Set and Feedback

Using introverted Intuiting requires that we go inside ourselves, empty our minds in a meditative or trancelike way, and discard our current sense of reality for a greater one. Can we accept that all our current conceptions are just convenient illusions? Transcending our own way of doing things requires that we keep concentrating on our inner aha moments until we get a universal perspective.

We know a realization is effective when it brings synergy—when the new perspective is greater than the sum of the old ones. These were all simply roads leading to a mountain peak. When a realization occurs and we reach a new peak, we have a tremendous feeling of power and wisdom.

Possible Misuses

Sometimes use of the introverted Intuiting process becomes rigid and dominating because of stress or because it is used without skill and without other processes to balance it. When this occurs, we may

- Find we can't stop thinking to relax—we experience a hyper-tense focus while mulling over a problem to get a solution
- Keep envisioning a specific fantastical image or keep having a particular scary dream
- Follow a system for thinking that is perceived by others as strange or inscrutable

- Overly focus on self-development at the expense of practical daily needs
- Be so focused on innovating or doing something in a novel way that we don't realize that really we're reinventing the wheel

Case Studies

The following vignettes illustrate introverted Intuiting. The first is an everyday situation and the second includes use with other processes in an organizational setting.

Case A

Thomas's friend has a grave concern after losing her job: what's in store for her in the future? It's not a problem that can be answered simply by asking an expert, looking in a book, or drawing on the past. Thomas quiets himself, emptying his mind. This involves going away from the conversation for a moment and ignoring anything known. He mentally wraps the question in a symbolic box, sends it off to the mysterious part of his mind, and moments later receives an answer that he gives to his surprised friend. Later that night, Thomas dwells on the question again before bed, sleeps on it, has a dream, and awakens the next morning with a more extensive and complex insight: a way to consider anyone's future.

Case B

Madeline runs transformational workshops for business executives. Sometimes she leads participants through a series of guided-imagery exercises, each one building on the previous one. She read about meditation exercises and experiments in consciousness and adapted them to the concerns of business executives. Participants often leave her workshops feeling that their minds have been rearranged and their bodies exhausted. Other times her style is very hands-off. She sets up a deceptively simple and fun group exercise and leaves the participants alone except to intervene by showing a symbol or reading a phrase that accurately mirrors what's going on and what will happen soon. Many leave saying, "It was amazing; you had to be there to understand." Madeline often exercises to help prepare beforehand, envisioning what will be needed and focusing inwardly on an image of how she needs to be.

Perspective Shifting

Here are some suggestions for how to communicate with, learn from, and influence someone who is using Introverted Intuiting.

- **Communicating to Build Rapport**
  - Ask what perspective the other person is coming from. The person may refer to a level, transformation, metamorphosis or viewpoint or use the word "perspective" with qualifiers like "higher," "broader," "global," or another term. Use this person's terms when you converse.
  - To gauge how the person feels about this metaperspective, ask whether considering different viewpoints is energizing or if the person feels lost in the situation. Use neutral, tentative language, such as "these various perspectives we might take" or "this greater perspective" as opposed to "your perspective."

- **Learning to Build New Skills**
  - Ask what viewpoints or ways of being are included under the person's metaperspective. Ask the person to describe these for you in terms of symbols, archetypes, prototypical situations, visual models, or images of the future.
  - Ask the person to describe what realizations or aha moments he or she has had. Ask how a hypothetical problem might be bypassed or reframed; watch as this person leaves the conversation or requests a day to think about it. What process does this person use, such as sleeping on it? And what tells the person soon after the realization how helpful it will likely be.

- **Influencing for Best Use**
  - How well does this metaperspective explain life? Ask the other person about a perspective he or she has had that he or she doesn't understand yet.
  - Ask how much this person has been able to go into a meditative mode and what mind shifting he or she might have left out or would like to engage again.

- **Helping to Discover New Outcomes**
  - Ask the person whether this metaperspective brings a new way of being. That is, how much does it really transform the situation? You may need to give examples of how others have undergone transformations.
  - If the person is dissatisfied, can he or she take a higher metaperspective that could bring synergizing results? (The person may not know what that higher metaperspective might be.)

There is always a future to realize
and a significance to be revealed.

Developing Introverted Intuiting

The following exercises will help you develop the process of introverted Intuiting. Get your self-assessment score from the beginning of this chapter and then set your starting point using the chart below.

If you scored	Then start with
0–3	The Introductory Exercises
4–9	The Basic Exercises
10+	The Advanced Exercises

As you work through the coming exercises, you may find some are particularly challenging. Include all the following steps to get more satisfying use of this process:

1. To access the process in the most effective way, withdraw from the world into a meditative mode. (See pages 166–167 to enter this mode.)

2. Access the core of the process: identify your current metaperspective—your different ways to see or be.

3. Engage in best-use activities, such as consulting your unconscious or dreams for a realization or working to achieve a transformation to fulfill what you envision.

4. Try for a desired outcome by selecting and shifting to the mindset or perspective that makes it happen.

5. Get feedback and calibrate: do differing viewpoints and ways to be enhance each other as you try them?

6. Integrate your use of introverted Intuiting with other cognitive processes (usually extraverted Thinking or extraverted Feeling).

As you develop this process, you'll be able to engage these steps all at once for increasingly coordinated and smooth use.

Introductory Exercises

These exercises will help you get comfortable engaging in a meditative mode to receive aha insights into questions and gain refreshed awareness.

CLEAR AND QUIET YOUR MIND

Find a quiet place. Shut out noise and add a soft, repetitive, neutral sound like a waterfall or drumming. Sit comfortably and focus inside yourself. Perhaps close your eyes. Empty your mind of thoughts and imagine a dark, empty space. Relax to maintain the emptiness, or focus on your breathing, a visual symbol, or a repetitive word to focus your attention. Only the potential of your own mind exists.

ASK A QUESTION AND LISTEN FOR AN ANSWER

Once you have cleared and quieted your mind, ask yourself a question about a current problem. Do not explore it. Just cast the question into the dark void of your mind. You may need to wait a few minutes. You might visualize a door: you can package your question, open the door, place the package beyond, and then close the door. The door will open at some point with a response, perhaps even during a later meditative session.

STAY WITH THE NEW AWARENESS

Focus on the response you receive when you listen for an answer. Welcome whatever emerges through the mental doorway. Allow yourself to pose any additional questions that come to mind, and speak with whatever lies beyond (this is your unconscious). After a time, this dialog will result in a metaperspective—and an unexpected and enlightening aha answer that closes the conversational door and leaves you feeling energized and refreshed. Upon reflection, this answer may easily be something you knew all along.

Basic Exercises

These exercises will help you get comfortable gaining and exploring metaperspectives, from sleeping on a problem in order to evoke an insight to engaging in dialog with symbols.

SLEEP ON A PROBLEM OR QUESTION

Pose a question or problem to yourself before going to bed. Let it be the last thought as you fall asleep. It could relate to a technical project or a personal relationship. When you awaken, lie in bed for a few minutes, clear your mind, and pose the question again. Insight may come quickly, or you may need to begin your day and find that an answer suddenly comes to mind, or you may need to keep returning to the question.

ENGAGE IN TRANCE ACTIVITY TO ATTAIN A REALIZATION

We become more receptive to the unconscious when engaged in trance-inducing activities. These activities include repetitive heavy exercise, being engaged with intense dance and music, or various martial art forms. Swimming, showering, or another experience of running water is often effective. Numerous forms of meditation involve emptying the mind or focusing on symbols or gestures to achieve a trance. All of these involve shutting out perception of the outer world and setting aside what we think is real. When engaging in a trance, remember to eliminate distracting sensory input; you will benefit most when you quiet and empty your mind. Trance activities are catalysts enabling us to enter a zone where we forget the problem or question we have posed to ourselves; then as we emerge from this mental zone, or as we move in and out of it, insights begin flooding the mind. These insights might be for ourselves or other people.

STAY WITH AHA MOMENTS

Whenever you experience a sudden realization or insight, stay with it and explore it. Consider what it means and what effect it will have on your life from today into the future. Keep a journal or notepad with you at all times to write down these surges of insight.

FOCUS YOUR ENERGIES TOWARD A VISION OF THE FUTURE

Create an image of how you would like to be or what you would like to happen in the future. The exact time frame is unimportant. Visualize yourself in the desired situation and then step into that self to see, hear, and feel as though you were there. You might draw a symbol or picture to represent this future. Keep focusing on the image. What do you hear, see, and feel? You are not trying to predict or to brainstorm. Just imagine a desired future and choose one or two qualities to dwell on, like a phrase you will hear from people or something remarkable you will see. Repeat this imaginative process to gather and focus all your energy and mental resources to help make the desired future happen.

EVOKE VARIOUS DEEP PERSPECTIVES

Ask a variety of people questions such as, "What you do think about the end of the universe?" or "Where do you think people go after they die?" Many people aren't keen to delve into these questions, so you might add, "Just tell me whatever comes to mind." Allow multiple responses. As you accumulate perspectives, you might write them down, share them with other people, or arrange them in a matrix, mandala, or other system that sets them in relation to each other to support this process. You will likely see blank spots in the matrix or mandala suggesting what to explore and consider further. Fill out the pattern so each perspective is fairly and fully represented. The result is a visual symbol of a metaperspective on your question.

SELECT SYMBOLS AS ASPECTS OF YOURSELF OR A SITUATION

Bring together in one place all the images and symbols that attract your attention. You can use symbols, totems, archetypes, or other abstractions to stand for various conflicting perspectives, ways to be, or aspects of yourself. When you were a child, what symbols or images attracted your interest? Perhaps dragons or cats? Also draw upon dream images. Or you can simply begin sketching on paper or surfing the Web, collecting images that draw your attention. Looking at renditions of the future or fantasy worlds is another quick way to tap into archetypical images. Iconic representations and other altered images can also be very powerful. Or visualize people you know and admire. The more an image holds your attention and the more you imagine it when it's not in front of you, the more powerful it is. You can even find new symbols within other symbols.

ENGAGE IN DIALOG WITH THE SYMBOLS

What do these symbols that you've collected say? Focus on each one, one at a time. What feelings and sensations come with each? Ask each symbol a question as if it were a person: "What do you represent?"

"What is your name or title?" "What can you do?" Just let words come to you, and allow the symbols to speak back as if they were real people. Engage in this process until the symbols begin using words you wouldn't normally use.

EXPLORE SYMBOLIC MEANINGS

After a dream, a symbolic dialog, or a vision of the future, meditate on the experience to get insights into its meanings. These meanings might be practical or metaphorical. Clear your mind to comprehend them. In a dream, you might find yourself at home but stuck on the first floor, unable to go upstairs, while something is climbing up from the darkness of the basement below. This might mean that you feel unable to progress in your life to the next level and you feel plagued by shadowy issues in the "basement" of your mind. These meanings can evoke questions and issues we normally don't attend to in daily life.

Advanced Exercises

These exercises will help you hone your basic use of the introverted Intuiting process, develop some advanced use, and learn to take a more active role in innovative projects and personal transformation.

GAIN INSIGHT FOR OTHERS

Questions and problems you present to your unconscious can be for or about anyone or anything. When you feel comfortable, ask someone if you can assist him or her. Listen for times when people wonder about the meaning of an experience or how the future will unfold. Consider helping people interpret their dreams (or their thoughts in general). If someone is wondering which option to pick when making a decision, submit each of their options to your unconscious and allow images to come into your mind that portray future results and implications for each one. When you notice someone's cognitive process, you might gently suggest other cognitive processes that might be useful.

REFRAME A SITUATION

When presented with conflicting perspectives, withdraw from the situation for a moment, quiet your mind, and use basic techniques to receive insight from the unconscious. Often the answer will not be a solution per se; you know it's a metaperspective if it eliminates the conflict. For example, if someone makes a comment that's not well received, the sudden aha solution you get could be an alternate interpretation of what was said. Reframing may take hours or days at first, but with practice you can withdraw from the moment and return with a reframe in a few moments. A reframe is not a snappy comeback. A reframe changes the meaning of the entire situation.

ENGAGE IN A CREATIVE PROJECT TO FOCUS YOURSELF

Do you admire someone or desire a skill? Catalyze change by concentrating your mind and energies on a transformative project like writing a book, learning a dance, starting a business, or raising a garden. The purpose isn't the project. The project acts as a focus, and the act of creating becomes a mirror and a guide on an inner journey of transformation. By completing the project you further complete yourself. As you concentrate on the project, keep visualizing the finished result. What will it look like? How will people respond to it? What qualities will it have? Where will it lead to next? How will it make you more successful? Choose one or two general but compelling outcomes. Feel, hear, and see yourself when the project is done. Immerse yourself in the image as if you were there and living it. This future should evoke a strong emotion like excitement or exhilaration, helping you complete the project to the best of your ability and thus make the image come true.

EVOKE YOUR DETAILED IMAGINATION

Look outside at a view such as your street. Ask yourself, what will this place become in the future? Allow yourself a vision of how it will look. Dwell on this imaginative view as if it's real. As you scan and move about the view, you may see people, artifacts, and activities you have never thought of before. You may even experience a sudden rush, seeing an entire world all at once in far more detail than you tend to notice in the real one around you. These details may include interrelationships, ideas, social structures, conflicts—everything typical of a world, highly cohesive and imaginary. Use a notepad, word processor, or tape recorder to capture everything you see in the view. Don't censor yourself or be concerned with accuracy. Just get it all down. You can also get more detail at any time in the future by recalling the image.

MERGE SYMBOLIC IMAGES

Whether concentrating on a project, engaging in dialog with symbols, or visualizing the future, you can merge various symbolic elements to synthesize new ones. Sit and hold out your hands, palms up. Focus on your left palm. Visualize one symbol. This might represent one version of you. See, hear, and feel the symbol. Now set that aside and focus on your right palm. Visualize, hear, and feel a second symbol. This might represent another version of you. Now set that aside and refocus on the left palm's image, and then return to the right again, and so on back and forth, switching slowly at first and then speeding up. At what feels like the right moment, bring your two palms together and merge the images.

ALLOW YOURSELF TO GIVE UP

Sometimes when you are waiting for insight, nothing comes. The mind stays quiet. This is natural. Stop focusing. Put the project, question, or image aside and engage in other activities, such as meeting with friends, taking a walk, or doing repetitive work, for example, cleaning or swimming. Keep a notepad or recorder with you for when an aha moment comes.

CHANGE YOURSELF TO FIT WHAT'S ENVISIONED

Consider an upcoming situation that demands peak performance, such as a social activity or team workshop. Visualize yourself next to an admired friend, a spirit animal, or a paragon of what's needed. Then merge the image of yourself with the image next to it to create a new self capable of handling the situation. With practice you can do this continuously in the background as you prepare normally for the activity. To manifest deep, lasting change, surround yourself with people and artifacts that have symbolic meaning to help focus and harness all your energies to achieve the desired transformation.

KEEP TRANSFORMING YOURSELF

You will know an insight or transformation is genuinely powerful when it brings synergy—when the new perspective or way to be is greater than the sum of the old ones. There is no mistaking the change. The metaperspective brings a new sense of self and new life options. Over time, trusted symbols and methods will wear out, especially if you ask them for insights on demand. So keep looking for new symbols and ways to focus yourself. Keep stepping through mental doorways to discover more doorways to change.

7

Measuring and Constructing for Progress

Understanding and Developing Extraverted Thinking

Benefits for Self-Leadership

As you develop extraverted Thinking, you will
- Be more efficient with time and resources
- Improve your ability to solve life's many problems in a practical, logical manner
- Stay objective when implementing difficult decisions
- Convince others with easy-to-follow reasoning

Assessing Current Development

Before continuing, check the phrases in the table that describe you well.

Part 1
☐ Usually know the time and what point you're at in a process.
☐ Determine success by measurement or other objective method, such as the time taken.
☐ Follow a straight line of reasoning.

Part 2
☐ Stick to making decisions based on impersonal measures, such as points earned.
☐ Conceive a comprehensive plan to maximize progress toward goals.

Part 3
☐ Mobilize resources and supervise implementation of a multipart plan.
☐ Construct an argument to convince someone using evidence clearly in front of you both.
☐ Lay out steps for others to complete tasks in time- and resource-efficient ways.

Scoring: Assign one point to items in part 1, two points to items in part 2, and three points to items in part 3.

Total points: [ ]

A score above nine indicates a likely preference for extraverted Thinking. A score from four to nine indicates a possible supporting preference or development from life experience. A score below four suggests a lack of development.

Understanding How Extraverted Thinking Works

At the core of extraverted Thinking is a measuring device. This might be a ruler or a stopwatch, a statistical test or a team progress report, sensory reality, a computer logic circuit, or anything else that can segment life into parts, whether minutes, project phases, urban zones, musical chords, discrete thoughts, or dollars spent. A template is also a measuring device. Much of what we have—calendars and cars, testing methods and next-day airmail, bridges and assembly lines—rely on measuring devices. When we can measure something, we can begin to control it.

Best-Use Activities

What can we do with a measuring device? We can determine how much of something we have or how similar two things are, as in comparing population growth with increases in food production. We can sort or order based on an indicator. Students are evaluated by test scores. Colors line up according to wavelengths of light. Vehicles made before a certain year are exempt from emissions tests. We set a threshold line or performance level and make decisions based on whether something crosses that line.

With quantification comes structure, repeatability, and expectation. Each morning the sun rises. Trade of goods for dollars is impersonal and predictable, as is a contract for actions by a certain date. Criteria like these make definitive boundaries and intervals. Students' final grades are based on points amassed instead of an instructor's whim, grudge, or favoritism. In this way, decisions are based on agreed-upon objective metrics and not on opinions.

When we enter new situations, we like to know the elements and the threshold points in order to make decisions based on how things are functioning. Situational demands often drive decisions. Each day we can apply discipline and schedule tasks based on a single gauge—time efficiency. We can gather data and see where the information naturally clumps by size, performance, or function and label it accordingly. We can also examine how well the components of a situation fit toward meeting a goal.

A grid, diagram, chart, set of boxes, or other system is useful for organizing qualities of objects, people, and even values. For example, we can use tangible qualities like color and hardness to sort backyard apples into three baskets for eating, pie making, or tossing in the rubbish bin. We can also give reasons for why we sorted and criteria for how we sorted.

We can line up or format our reasoning and actions using a template. A template, like a sewing pattern or preformatted document, can be used as a guide to replicate or judge something. We follow the template to produce a result. A template can be an entire methodology for implementing a procedure, such as the instructions for using a tool or replicating an experiment. Just as we can pick out a best-fit line from a

FIG. 7.1. Cognitive snapshot of extraverted thinking

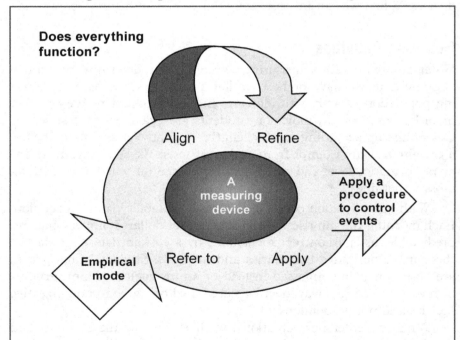

At the core of extraverted Thinking is a measuring device, such as a stopwatch or a progress report. When we go into an empirical mode, we rely only on explicit measures and templates (ways to format) to make decisions. We can refer to, align, refine, and apply a measuring device. Applying often means using a procedure to control events. We reflect on our metrics by asking, does everything function well?

set of data points and project an outcome, so too can we use the "data points" from experiences to create procedures. When we evaluate what's shown to us, a template can indicate what's missing, out of sequence, or not on point, and we can synchronize people's activities to reach a goal. We can create new templates by following more general ones, combining existing templates in a modular way, or copying one of nature's many examples. The world is full of examples that provide us with rules of thumb for what works.

Empirical reasoning means to assert or verify based on observation or experiment. Claims that align with computable facts or with a template are viewed as logical and reasonable. To the extent that emotions, social relations, and personal impressions can be sorted or measured and labeled, they are accepted. If we don't understand how a decision was made, we can progressively step back to get views of how things are arranged at different scales (for example, houses, cities, and planets).

People who prefer extraverted Thinking draw on expectations about the meaning of measurements to maintain order as they navigate life and make sense of all aspects of living.

Mind-Set and Feedback

Using extraverted Thinking requires us to be empirical, focusing on and trusting what is visible or measurable. We must be ready to make or accept decisions based on objective gauges, regardless of feelings or individual values. Measurement leads to control, whether the measuring device is a vote-counting system or a government economic intervention. Sometimes we are in charge and sometimes we are not; this fact is viewed as reality and is not taken personally.

The effectiveness of a methodology, an assessment, or a heuristic can be determined by checking whether everything functions correctly, achieves a performance level, or provides us with control. When things line up, we find a tremendous feeling of rightness and progress.

Possible Misuses

Sometimes use of the extraverted Thinking process becomes rigid and dominating because of stress or because it is used without skill and without other processes to balance it. When this occurs, we may

- Receive feedback suggesting that we are overplanning or telling others what to do too much

- Feel bound by the clock, perhaps trying too hard to optimize our tasks and not accounting sufficiently for the unexpected
- Feel that certain things should or should not be thought. Perhaps we are perceived as argumentative as we correct mistakes
- Find ourselves engaging in repetitious behavior, such as excessive reorganizing
- Forget Einstein's wisdom: not everything that counts in life can be counted, and not everything that can be counted counts

Case Studies

The following vignettes illustrate extraverted Thinking. The first is an everyday situation and the second includes use with other processes in an organizational setting.

Case A

Brett writes a regular editorial column. Today he is writing on a local community issue. He prepares by checking whether an opponent's statements line up with the evidence. His opponent is arguing that some one-way streets are needed to improve pedestrian safety, and Brett is all for keeping the streets safe. However, his opponent apparently hasn't considered all the consequences of his proposal since the  changes will increase traffic elsewhere. Anyone can see this by looking at a map. Also, no objective criteria exist since no one has been tracking accidents or complaints. Brett gathers data from adjacent communities; even a generous evaluation doesn't come close to his opponent's assertions. He uses his article to point out these problems and to outline a more workable solution.

Case B

Jean, a hospital administrator, is charged with monitoring the success of a new employee relations program. Employees are already sorted by role: staff, nurses, doctors, and administrators. Each role includes different activities, so Jean could devise survey questions based on roles, but the underlying

metrics would not be the same and different measures can't be easily combined or compared. She considers measuring time efficiency, but this is too impersonal for her; she believes in a humane hospital. Another criterion is not wasting people's time. She decides to ask employees three simple questions each week about time, motivation, and results. The responses can be sorted to create a graph to show the hospital board every two weeks.

Perspective Shifting

Here are some suggestions for how to communicate with, learn from, and influence someone who is using extraverted Thinking.

- **Communicating to Build Rapport**
  - Ask what metric or template the other person is using. The person may refer to a progress report, time frame, methodology, operation, program, agenda, test, performance level, heuristic, interval, or evidence visible to everyone. Use this person's terms when you converse.
  - To gauge how the person feels about using the metric, ask if an activity is wasting his or her time or seems like time well spent. Be straightforward and avoid personal opinions (statements that haven't been or can't be evaluated empirically). If you mention feelings, refer to them as "one of the factors."

- **Learning to Build New Skills**
  - Find out what the metric or template includes. Ask the person to describe these for you in terms of steps, categories, units, parts, elements, departments, lists, diagrams, flowcharts, and so on.
  - Ask the person to describe his or her reasoning process. What indicates which measure or procedure to use? How does the person calibrate data gathered to be sure it's accurate? For example, when doing interviews, how are the interviews structured and what checks are in place for honesty? What will indicate whether the results can be trusted in making a decision?

- **Influencing for Best Use**
  - Consider how well these metrics are predicting and controlling for what is happening. Ask the person what he or she would like to get a measure of but so far has been unable to measure.
  - Ask how often the person has been able to go into an empirical mode and how much time he or she has devoted to revising the reasoning or procedures in light of data and test results.

- **Helping to Discover New Outcomes**
  - Ask the other person how much control the metric or methodology is really giving over the situation. For comparison, you may need to use facts, figures, charts, and some logical reasoning and provide examples of other documented approaches that have worked.
  - If the person is dissatisfied, will another measuring device, methodology, or operating procedure work? (The person may not know what that new tool might be.)

Everything and everyone can be
logical, structured, and organized.

Developing Extraverted Thinking

The following exercises will help you develop the extraverted Thinking process. Get your self-assessment score from the beginning of this chapter and then set your starting point using the chart below.

If you scored	Then start with
0–3	The Introductory Exercises
4–9	The Basic Exercises
10+	The Advanced Exercises

As you work through the coming exercises, you may find some are particularly challenging. Include all the following steps to get more satisfying use of this process:

1. To access the process in the most effective way, go into a impersonal empirical mode. (See pages 166–167 to enter this mode.)

2. Access the core of the process: which metric or template will you use to assess the situation and make progress?

3. Engage in best-use activities, such as sorting, breaking something down into steps or parts, assigning benchmark values, or monitoring a procedure.

4. Try for a desired outcome by comparing measured progress against benchmarks of success. Are you or the team in control?

5. Get feedback and calibrate: are you meeting milestones and is everything running according to plan?

6. Integrate your use of extraverted Thinking with other cognitive processes (usually introverted Sensing or introverted Intuiting).

As you develop this process, you'll be able to engage these steps all at once for increasingly coordinated and smooth use.

Introductory Exercises

These exercises will help you get comfortable making decisions based on measurable evidence, probable consequences, and optimal functionality.

CHOOSE A SPACE TO ORGANIZE

Over time, beloved junk tends to accumulate—in our homes, in our offices, and everywhere we spend time. Often we keep things we don't really use or need. Choose a room in your house, your office, or other work area to clean out—even a collection of files and folders on a computer. Be prepared to throw things away from now on.

DECIDE ON SORTING CRITERIA

Scan the space you have chosen to organize, noting the qualities and quantities of items before you, mentally sorting them by similarities and differences. For example, you will likely put all small office supplies in one drawer and large ones in a cabinet. Also consider how often you have used items over a period of time, such as the last year. If you have excess items, set a strict rule like keeping only what you use everyday and any heirlooms. Consider storage, trash, or charity for everything else. Set up what you'll need beforehand, such as bins. If you need only one item and you have ten or more, then you can keep two and get rid of the rest. Dispose of outdated items like old newspapers. For special items, set rules for genuine value, such as gifts from family members or close friends. You can organize these items into one place, such as a display cabinet or a private desk drawer. Set all of these rules—your decision-making process—before you start to organize.

SORT EMPIRICALLY

Sort your chosen space using the rules you set. You will likely encounter unexpected conditions requiring ad hoc decisions, which is fine. Arrange items for efficient use of space, and use the natural limits of containers and the room to help you make these decisions. If you have an extra drawer toward the end of the job and there are some random items you would like to keep, then choose some of the items to keep in the drawer.

Basic Exercises

These exercises will help you get comfortable measuring and constructing procedures for progress, from optimal use of time to setting criteria and representing data visually.

OPTIMIZE USE OF TIME

Create a to-do list. Indicate the time likely needed to complete each task. If you're not sure, then review past experiences, ask or observe others, or compare a current task to a similar task—then take an average. If any variation is likely—such as a traffic jam while running an errand—note that. Now assign a numeric value for how urgent the activity is, where you need to be, what resources you need, and the frame of mind you need to be in for each task. Now "min-max" (optimize) by urgency, time, and similarity of resources or tools used.

DETERMINE HOW TO COMPLETE A TASK

If you are not sure how to accomplish a task or solve a problem, you have several options. Ask others for examples of how they handle it. They might show you, but having them write down the steps will simplify duplicating the process. Or pick two or three similar past experiences and either mix and match elements or find an average. Alternatively, look at nature's many examples. An ant colony exemplifies how to run a complex operation—up to a point. For handling tasks requiring more than a few hours, and perhaps weeks or more, break down what's needed into manageable units of three hours or less. Always allow fifty minutes to three hours to complete a task, such as cleaning a room or writing a paper. This time frame balances the brain's attention span versus what's needed to complete most projects. To save time, glance over what's needed and do one segment of a project, then use what you've done as a template to complete the remaining segments.

SET MEASURABLE THRESHOLD CRITERIA

To evaluate how you or others are doing, set measurable criteria, such as time taken, dollars spent, or percent performance. Consider available assessment tools. To evaluate performance, priority, or another outcome, look for past statistics or assign numeric weights. Set dividing lines between evaluation categories based on observation, examples, need, or clear differences, such as optional versus required steps. For example, anything under 2 percent could be considered negligible; amounts under 20 percent, rare; 50 percent, average; 80 percent, common; and 98 percent or more, always true. Analyze the data to see how well what's being evaluated passes the criteria. If it doesn't pass, look to see how far you have to go.

QUANTIFY SUBJECTIVE DATA
Qualitative data can be represented numerically. For example, some employees might have difficult client cases, making them look less productive in terms of total cases completed. To represent this, consider a new measure, such as case difficulty, then establish criteria and calculate the numbers. When establishing criteria, look at criteria from similar situations, ask others, or look for distinct differentiators, such as clients who get emotional represent difficult cases.

REPRESENT DATA VISUALLY
Represent data visually in a graph, or use a matrix for qualitative data. Look for clumps or thresholds. For example, when examining employee productivity, you might see distinct groupings. These groupings will likely not be perfectly distinct, but they represent dividing lines, such as when selecting employees for raises.

LOOK AT RATE OF CHANGE OVER TIME
It's useful to gather data to see how a situation changes over time. You can see trends, such as increasing or decreasing cash flow or birthrates. Look at the rate of change—perhaps a rate of increase is decreasing over time. Long-term cycles are common, such as downturns in the stock market at the start of each decade. Look at long-term trends to ameliorate bad news and to keep seemingly good news in perspective.

SEGMENT BY COMPONENTS AND FUNCTIONALITY
Consider the structural components and possible functions of an everyday object like a chair. A typical chair has four legs, a seat, and a back. Now consider the typical user of that chair, say, in an office. Is the chair a convenient height? Does its back adequately support the typical user? Are components present that don't serve a function? The point is not whether the chair matches you or someone else personally. The point

is to evaluate an object, situation, line of reasoning, or work position based on its structural components and functionality. Evaluation might involve measurement against a criterion, such as efficient use of time. Ideally, a minimal number of components yield a maximal number of efficient functions.

Advanced Exercises

These exercises will help you hone the basic use of this process and develop some advanced use. Learn to take a more active role in creating procedures and forming arguments.

GATHER DATA TO CREATE A PROCEDURE

If you know how to perform a task, then document your process and streamline it to the simplest step-by-step procedure. Also interview others with similar experience and create an aggregate of everyone's input. Others may have encountered factor-specific situations and solutions. In your procedure, mention contingencies for common events and mention the likelihood of each. Backup plans are always useful.

DECIDE HOW TO FOLLOW OR PLACE STEPS

When breaking down a task, you'll see two kinds of steps: those that are critical to the final outcome and those that are optional. Look at which steps are prerequisites for others. Include substeps and decision points to return to earlier points. For tasks that require multiple actions at once, such as using two hands to hammer a nail, segment the directions (such as by left hand and right hand) and include a diagram. Similarly, when following directions, scrutinize the directions to locate prerequisites and other major points to reference later as needed. When organizing other people to follow steps toward a goal, also consider the methods you'll use to synchronize activities, resource use, prerequisites, and possible consequences.

GRAPH CONSEQUENCES AND ESTIMATE OUTCOMES

List possible outcomes and assign numbers to reflect the percent likelihood of each, based on experience or similar situations. You can do this by starting with now and looking ahead, noting branches based on typical events that can happen. Assign percent chances to each branch and final possible rewards, and then mentally calculate the most likely best path or paths.

CREATE A NEW ASSESSMENT TOOL

If you need a measure and current tools won't do, then create a new tool. For example, to assess employees' satisfaction, create a questionnaire. Draw from existing knowledge, questionnaires, and observations. Keep the questionnaire short, simple, and relevant, and use everyday language. Then gather data and evaluate it by comparing it to observed behavior and other data points. Analyze and graph the data as necessary to see results and what doesn't fit your observations. Remember when gathering evidence to consider common categories and criteria needed for a statistical test (such as equal numbers of each gender).

CREATE AN OBJECTIVE CONTRACT

For handling disputes, get the facts straight, hear each argument and goal, and create a contract with the optimal payoff for each party. Break the situation into parts that can be evaluated for worth or consequences. This helps people negotiate in a structured, impersonal way. The contract can be verbal or written in clear, everyday language. The method for evaluating fulfillment should be impersonal and measurable by all—someone will do a task by a certain date or a result will happen. If needed, the contract can be adjusted contingent on possible events.

EXAMINE ARGUMENTS IN DEPTH

When dealing with arguments, first remove value judgments, spin, and bias and line them up against facts and common criteria. For example, adjectives are red lights indicating value statements. Spin refers to selective emphasis on some facts or consequences while ignoring others. Opinions are statements that are unsupported by evidence. Examine if stated likelihoods match real examples. Beware arguments that appeal to values. Are there underlying assumptions, such as everyone should get along or one should trust experts? Compare underlying assumptions to the evidence at hand. If something is unclear, ask for facts, metrics or criteria used, results obtained, and similar known cases, and assess whether facts were gathered in a documented way by a neutral party. A thorough examination of facts and consequences often reveals empty arguments.

WEIGH MULTIPLE FACTORS

When examining a situation, list all observable causal factors, noting their degree of influence on the situation and on each other. You might separate out major factors from minor factors. For a thorough understanding, consider the likelihood that certain factors could be changed, multiple ways one might change them, the likely impact of each factor, and any optimal factor. For example, if an analysis of data gathered about employee productivity reveals that early broad intense training is better than later retraining but retraining is less expensive, you might be able to find a balance to get an optimal result.

MAINTAIN EMOTIONAL OBJECTIVITY

If you start getting emotional at an inopportune time, you can reestablish objectivity in several ways. You can withdraw from the situation and perhaps write instead of speak about it. Or you can step outside your body. Visualize the problematic scene as if you are a fly on the wall or watching the whole scene on a movie screen. If this isn't enough distance, then step back further, such as imagining yourself in the theater projection booth, watching yourself in the audience, watching yourself on screen.

KEEP UPDATING CRITERIA

When a procedure or criterion isn't working, such as a method for accepting or rejecting potential new projects, consider alternative methods and metrics. With each one, look all the way down the line and map out possible consequences, such as percent chance of success versus possible payoff. For example, if a slight lowering of test standards will drastically improve high school graduation rates, we might be tempted to adjust the standard to save grief and money. However, it is worth the time to examine likely ripple effects—such as a possible surge in state college costs—to avoid "passing the buck." For example, if entering college students are performing poorly and the college administrators have no say in secondary education, then it's unfair to pass the problem on to them if they don't have the resources to handle it.

MIN-MAX ALL ASPECTS OF YOUR LIFE

Repeat all methods and steps above in all areas of your life to get the maximum rational results for the minimum use of time, space, talent, and other resources. At the least, you and others you organize will accomplish much.

Gaining Leverage Using a Framework

Understanding and Developing Introverted Thinking

Benefits for Self-Leadership

As you develop introverted Thinking, you will
- Think in a clearer, more consistent way
- Greatly deepen your expertise in a particular discipline
- Efficiently solve problems using pinpoint leverage (subtle influence)
- Better understand life's many principles

Assessing Current Development

Before continuing, check the phrases in the table that describe you well.

Part 1
☐ Accurately reference a framework, such as a scientific theory or philosophical principle.
☐ Be guided by a logical perspective, theory, or other nugget of reasoning.
☐ Detach yourself to analyze a situation from various angles.

Part 2
☐ Take apart something to figure out the principles on which it works.
☐ Easily reference multiple frameworks at once while problem solving.

Part 3
☐ Use leverage points to get the maximum effect with minimal effort.
☐ Analyze and critique something to reconcile what doesn't fit with a framework's principles.
☐ Fine-tune a definition or concept to support a theory, perspective, or framework.

Scoring: Assign one point to items in part 1, two points to items in part 2, and three points to items in part 3.

Total points: 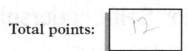 12

A score above nine indicates a likely preference for introverted Thinking. A score from four to nine indicates a possible supporting preference or development from life experience. A score below four suggests a lack of development.

Understanding How Introverted Thinking Works

At the core of introverted Thinking is a <u>ruling framework</u>. The framework might be a scientific theory or taxonomy, a way to look at a particular class of problems, a set of defined sales techniques, a philosophical perspective, a principle of human relationships, or anything else with definitions, categories, and logical principles and criteria. A framework is general. That is, for the phenomena it describes, it applies to and governs any specific situation that arises. Physics describes motion regardless of what's moving. The framework enables understanding in all categorically similar situations by logical deduction. There are many frameworks.

Best-Use Activities

What can we do with a ruling framework? We can reference it, fit observations into it, analyze and clarify situations according to it, and critique something with respect to it. Perhaps someone we talk to equates two things that rightly belong to different categories, and we respond by giving the definitions we know. Dolphins are not fish because they fit the category of mammals though they live in the sea. Or we suggest a framework to help someone gain insight and get to the heart of a problem.

When we aren't clear on the underlying principles of something, we might take it apart as we analyze it to more precisely observe its elements and their interrelationships. This can mean literally disassembling a device or mentally dissecting an idea. This can be an exciting process as we figure out a mystery and find new angles from which to look at it. Each analysis is an opportunity to clarify our framework and to extend it into new areas. A geologist analyzes rocks found together, deduces a sediment pattern, and maybe refines her understanding of erosion. Sometimes a new mental model is needed for a new kind of situation, or we run into an idea that has merit but is in need of some adjustment. We can design, adapt, clarify, refine, and shift a framework, although these processes may take a long time as we carefully consider all the angles. A manager might reconcile differing teamwork principles over many projects. We can fit differing frameworks together to bring them into alignment.

A framework will often suggest leverage points from which to fix a problem or make a change. How can we maximize explanatory power with minimum complexity? How can we best coordinate our next move with the situation? A leverage point might be a single word or an action of pinpoint precision to solve the problem.

As we observe a problem, we fit observations to a framework, perhaps explicitly naming and labeling phenomena as they occur. We may labor to locate just the right term to most accurately and succinctly define or describe what we observe, and we may appropriate common

FIG. 8.1. Cognitive snapshot of introverted thinking

Is the framework elegant?

Align   Refine

A ruling framework

Use leverage to solve a problem

Observer mode   Refer to   Apply

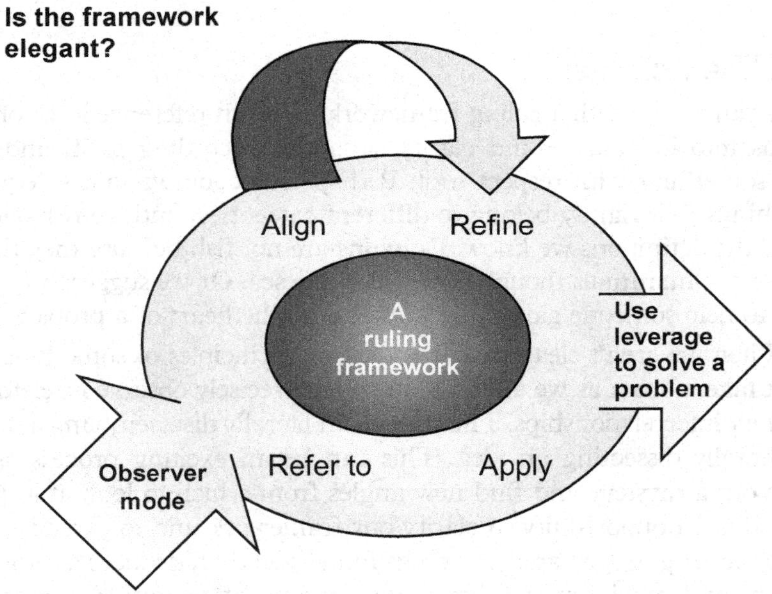

At the core of introverted Thinking is a ruling framework, such as a scientific theory or philosophical principle. When we go into an observer mode, we detach ourselves from the situation under study so we can use the framework without bias. We can refer to, align, refine, and apply a framework. Applying often means using leverage to solve a problem. We reflect on our framework by asking, is the framework elegant?

terms to exactly capture the categories we find. For example, physicists refer to the "flavor" of subatomic particles. When presented with an idea, we may analyze and critique it to eliminate what doesn't fit with the principles of the framework we know. A company's growth strategy might be examined and judged by how well it fits with our underlying mental model of corporate performance. We maintain consistency with the framework and its underlying principles over a long period of time. It holds even when superficial evidence or a competing, less rigorous theory suggests otherwise. We—and likely others—have carefully refined the framework, perhaps over years of informed observation. Data only informs reasoning.

An elegant framework is one that gets to the core or essence of our observations, bringing deep understanding and expertise with minimal complexity. A framework should be precise, logical, and consistent, with corollaries derived from clearly defined axioms and stated assumptions. If we stipulate that "people are born good," then we can decide on many social policies from education to criminal punishment. To handle exceptions, we refine our definition of "good." These characteristics require continuous refining and ever-finer distinctions in the definitions of principles. The framework is considered effective if it's accurate, and beautiful in its elegant simplicity if it's universal.

People who prefer introverted Thinking rely on their mental frameworks to navigate life and make sense of all aspects of living.

Mind-Set and Feedback

Using introverted Thinking requires that we go into an observer mode—that we become objective and impersonal. To be accurate and general we must step away from a situation and become detached so we don't contaminate our analysis with personal values, biases, and life situations. A scientific framework, for example, doesn't belong to any one person. It is a tool we can use to describe a phenomenon. It accurately represents what's observed.

The soundness of a framework can be decided according to the timeless modeling principles of elegance and simplicity. Inadequacy here may suggest a need for refinement and clarification. When a framework is elegant, we have a tremendous feeling of clarity and truth.

Possible Misuses

Sometimes use of the introverted Thinking process becomes rigid and dominating because of stress or because it is used without skill and without other processes to balance it. When this occurs, we may

- Feel sure that something can't exist or can't possibly be true because it doesn't fit a specific criterion or principle
- Find it hard to accept evidence that contradicts our mental framework, perhaps even when data is clear-cut
- Overspecialize and perhaps overapply our specialized framework to all aspects of life
- Appear to others as calculating, ridiculing, or uncaring in our interactions, even when we don't intend those attitudes at all
- Provide criticism and find it difficult to offer suggestions for improvement

Case Studies

The following vignettes illustrate introverted Thinking. The first is an everyday situation and the second includes use with other processes in an organizational setting.

Case A

Karen knows a lot about how cars work. Her friend mentions a problem he's having. Karen hasn't opened the hood of this particular model car before, but based on her internal mental framework of car design and function, she observes and then correctly classifies the problem, identifies the likely parts involved, and suggests a solution that is based on the  framework. From Karen's perspective, she has a detached, objective, scientific understanding of the universal operating principles of cars and is matching the situation to what she knows. Later, when her own car has a very unusual problem, the garage mechanic suggests a cause, but Karen soon determines this can't be right when he confuses the function of a part.

Case B

John is a trained anthropologist and currently assists organizations in adjusting their cultures. He applies several mental models at once as he observes an organization from many perspectives. His aim is often to look for key leverage points from which to shift the culture of a company or group while honoring its need for cost savings and bottom-line results. A  change in organizational culture can often mean positive results for many people—from employees to managers, executives, and customers. When John recently encountered a particularly subtle problem at an organization, he described his observations to several respected peers. Later, after observing the outcome of his work with the organization, he made a refinement to the basic framework he uses and shared it with his peers in an academic article.

Perspective Shifting

Here are some suggestions for how to communicate with, learn from, and influence someone who is using Introverted Thinking.

- **Communicating to Build Rapport**
  - Ask what ruling framework the other person is using. The person may refer to a tool, technique, method, model, principle, strategy, theory, formula, or criterion. Use this person's term when you converse.
  - To gauge how the person feels about using the framework, ask whether he or she has clarity or is feeling some confusion about aspects of the situation. Use detached language, such as "the model" or "this principle" as opposed to "your model."

- **Learning to Build New Skills**
  - Ask about the framework's core principles and assumptions. Ask the person to describe for you the categories and definitions he or she is using. Or ask what criteria are being used to apply a particular principle.

- Ask the person to describe what leverage points he or she sees and to demonstrate the use of a leverage point to shift the situation. Look for what this person does before and right after this demonstration. What clues did he or she observe the moment before acting? And what clues did he or she observe afterward that indicated responses to the change?

- **Influencing for Best Use**
  - How well do the observations fit the framework? Ask the person to describe the data that is being left out because it doesn't fit.
  - Ask how much the person has been able to go into an observer mode and what angles he or she might have missed or would like to take a look at again.

- **Helping to Discover New Outcomes**
  - Ask the other person whether the devised solution is as elegant as it could be. That is, does it really get to the essence of the situation? You may need to give examples of others with expertise who've gotten to the core of a problem.
  - If the person is dissatisfied, could another ruling framework provide an elegant solution? (The person may not know what that new framework might be.)

Everything can be explained and understood
in terms of its underlying principles.

Developing Introverted Thinking

The following exercises will help you develop the introverted Thinking process. Get your self-assessment score from the beginning of this chapter and then set your starting point using the chart below.

If you scored	Then start with
0–3	The Introductory Exercises
4–9	The Basic Exercises
10+	The Advanced Exercises

As you work through the coming exercises, you may find some are particularly challenging. Include all the following steps to get more satisfying use of this process:

1. To access the process in the most effective way, go into a detached observer mode. (See pages 166–167 to enter this mode.)
2. Access the core of the process: which ruling framework is appropriate for solving the problem?
3. Engage in best-use activities, such as fitting observations into the framework to determine the nature of the problem and a desired outcome.
4. Try for a desired outcome using one or more leverage points to solve the problem.
5. Get feedback and calibrate: are the framework and the solution elegant in efficient simplicity and consistent design?
6. Integrate your use of introverted Thinking with other cognitive processes (usually extraverted Sensing or extraverted Intuiting).

As you develop this process, you'll be able to engage these steps all at once for increasingly coordinated and smooth use.

Introductory Exercises

These exercises will help you get comfortable observing and dealing with situations according to a principle as you observe and solve problems every day.

EXPLORE A PRINCIPLE

Consider a principle, such as survival of the fittest or the golden rule. Look up information about this principle, such as common corollaries and ways it has been defined by various thinkers. For example, survival of the fittest implies selection between competitors and suggests that, in the animal kingdom, making random moves is a powerful way to defeat competitors' strategies.

OBSERVE THE PRINCIPLE IN ACTION

Spend a day observing, fitting what you see to the principle you've been exploring. With survival of the fittest, you might observe how individuals behave in groups as well as how groups themselves might compete or even how ideas compete with each other in a cultural arena. Some observation may be direct, and some may involve looking up data and reading case studies and analyses by experts. Observation will require you to make distinctions. You might pick out two opposing sports teams as clear competitors; however, consider that a married couple, when dealing with their children, can be viewed as competitors. View everything, as much as you can, with an eye toward understanding it in terms of the principle.

CONSIDER A MOVE WITH THE PRINCIPLES IN MIND

Be open to an opportunity to apply the principle. This might mean offering others an interpretation or proposing a course of action. Following survival of the fittest, you might suggest resolving a dispute through a game, or you might act randomly when someone challenges you. Observe the degree of effectiveness of your action. What about intended versus unexpected effects? You may want to review the principle in more detail before trying again.

Basic Exercises

These exercises will help you get comfortable using a framework, from learning definitions and making distinctions to fitting and explaining observations and critiquing others' ideas.

CHOOSE A FRAMEWORK

The framework you choose might be a philosophy, a scientific model, or any discipline that has an abstract or theoretical side. One example is music theory. Another is the function, design, operation, and repair of vehicles. The principles of drama are a framework for effective fiction writing that transcends genre, style, plot, or other specifics. Yet another example is a customer service and employee management framework. A framework is more than a principle; it is a lens, a language, and a tool all in one for understanding the world. Frameworks are often described in books or referred to as rules, such as "the three rules of sales success."

RESEARCH THE FRAMEWORK

Locate the leading experts in the field of your framework. Expertise isn't determined only by diplomas, institutional affiliation, or title, so you will need to read several different perspectives from different experts and judge for yourself, noting what the experts' peers have to say as well as how clearly and elegantly the ideas are represented.

EVALUATE THE FRAMEWORK FOR ELEGANCE

Timeless principles apply to evaluating frameworks. The core criterion is how well the framework describes many observed phenomena. The more accurately it can describe and predict a situation, and the less cluttered and complex the model, the better the framework. Other criteria include how well defined the framework is and how many rich deductions can be made from it. A powerful framework suggests ways to intervene and change situations.

LEARN THE FRAMEWORK IN DEPTH

Learning your framework in depth will take time and experience, but there is no substitute for thoroughly learning as much as you can from the start. Learn the specialized terminology, definitions, and categories. For example, if you are learning about monetary investment, you need to learn about rates of return and kinds of investment options. Learning more often involves getting your hands dirty—for example, opening up the hood of your car—or you may rely on your imagination to explore the framework. You also might get training in a workshop.

FIT OBSERVATIONS TO THE FRAMEWORK

Observe a situation and try applying the framework to it. Try many different angles as you begin to understand the situation in terms of the definitions, categories, and principles you've learned. You might watch over time and perhaps document what you see, just as an anthropologist patiently observes, records, and reviews. Consider writing or speaking about what you've observed and how the model applies to the situation. Explaining is often an aid to deeper understanding, and it will challenge you to find the most precise and accurate terms.

BEGIN TO APPLY THE FRAMEWORK

Review definitions and concepts relating to the framework. Eliminate contextual variation. This means to abstract from what's observed. For example, you might consider people as simple shapes and their interactions as relational arrows. Try out possible explanations in the same way you would try on pairs of shoes until you find the one that fits best. You are using the framework as a tool to interpret the situation, so look from different angles as you make logical deductions. You can also go with the closest fit and begin applying, or imagining, a solution to see what happens.

SET ASIDE WHAT DOESN'T FIT FOR LATER INQUIRY

Don't expect all aspects of a situation to fit the model exactly. Remember the principle of Occam's razor: the simplest explanation that covers the most aspects is probably the best one. Some aspects of what you see are invariably addressed by other frameworks, which you might also like to learn eventually to explain what doesn't fit. For example, if you're trying to understand human evolution in terms of geography and climate and you run into something unexplainable, then consider reading up on the role of hormones and traditional diets. Similarly, while it's sometimes possible to explain absolutely everything about a situation in terms of the framework, be careful that your perception isn't narrowed by the framework to the point that you no longer notice what doesn't fit.

Keep unusual data in an "other" category for possible future review, for use in clarifying and refining your understanding, or for use in bringing other frameworks into alignment with the one you're using.

CRITIQUE OTHERS WITH THE FRAMEWORK IN MIND

With sufficient expertise, you can address others' interpretations and frameworks. If you're immersing yourself in economic theory and you read about a new government policy, you can evaluate the policy in terms of the theory, pointing out specifically where there is contradiction or confusion. The framework, as an overlay, will immediately reveal what doesn't follow or fit. Now critique yourself to align your actions and thoughts with a model.

Advanced Exercises

These exercises will help you hone your basic use of the introverted Thinking process and develop some advanced use. Learn to take a more active role in finding and applying leverage and using models.

LOCATE THE LEVERAGE POINTS

What is leverage? Consider how physical leverage works. Imagine a flat piece of paper on a desk. As you slowly slide the paper off, it first remains flat, then dips over the edge, and then falls off. It has a tipping point. Now repeat this process, but add a paper clip. The paper clip has a stabilizing effect if it's placed on the part of the paper that's on the desk. Conversely, it has a catalytic destabilizing effect if it's placed on the part of the paper that's off the desk. Now consider the framework you're using and what it has to offer for finding solutions. What leverage points, tipping points, and tools does it suggest regarding a solution?

CONSIDER APPLYING LIGHT LEVERAGE

To continue with the analogy above, you might slowly—almost imperceptibly—slide the paper. This is slow, patient application. Maybe you want to influence other people's ideas and overcome their resistance to your idea; you might slowly and patiently present them with small examples and slight pressure until they suddenly change their minds on their own. Now consider the framework you are using and how you can apply leverage this way.

CONSIDER APPLYING STRONG LEVERAGE

Another kind of leverage involves introducing a metaphorical paper clip to a situation. Where can you place the smallest possible paper clip to suddenly stabilize or alter the situation? What are the minimal resources you need for pinpoint precision? For example, you might persuade someone to consider your idea by offering a small yet tempting incentive. Many businesses do this to get customers in their doors. Now consider the framework you're using and how you can apply leverage this way.

CONSIDER APPLYING INDIRECT LEVERAGE

What can you do when a problem won't budge? For example, a facilitator might have a difficult group and decide to try to move it along by mixing subtle and strong strategies. Using the previous analogy, you could place the paper clip in an apparent stabilizing position but right near the edge of the desk, so only a small push is needed to make the paper fall. Now consider the framework you're using and how you can apply leverage this way.

APPLY THE PRINCIPLE OF LEVERAGE

Consider what you've learned about leverage and try it out in some real-life situations. Take the time to observe the situation first. What is the paper? What is the paper clip? What is the desk? And what could it mean to move the paper or for the paper to fall? Work it out in your mind and then try your ideas out. Consider all the factors and look for different potential moves and the options or possibilities that may appear after those moves. What can you do with the least effort for the greatest effect?

RESEARCH OTHERS' FRAMEWORKS

Most situations involve other people. People have their own frameworks and often notice different aspects of a situation, and they often appear to be competing either for the same outcome for themselves or for a different kind of outcome altogether. What are people's agendas and frameworks? You could observe, watching to see what definitions they reference and what leverage points they apply. However, most people don't think in terms of frameworks and leverage, at least not consciously, so in a sense you are simply evaluating how well they know and can apply the framework you are using. Similarly, not everything useful or relevant is visible to everyone. Potential outcomes and tools may not be obvious. Consider that others may see things you don't. Observe them. If they are talking about or looking at something that doesn't make sense to you, then focus on observing their thinking and behavior, or ask what framework they are using.

LEARN TO REFOCUS ATTENTION

You can influence attention. In a competitive situation, such as trying to improve your standing against a rival business, it's often wise to keep vital information to yourself. In a helping role, you might help your children study better by removing distractions. To help you or others focus, you can hide part of a situation when applying leverage. Or you can introduce a reward or other new element to a situation. Timing can make all the difference.

WORK WITH OTHERS USING AN ETHICAL FRAMEWORK

You can get synergistic results working with others, particularly when everyone can trust and coordinate with each other through shared information and outcomes. Multiple people apply multiple leverage points at once to transform companies, economies, and cultures. The physician's principle "First, do no harm" and The Platinum Rule® (give unto others what they want to receive) are universal time-tested principles for creating win-win situations for everyone.

USE MULTIPLE FRAMEWORKS

Over the ages and throughout nature there have been many kinds of situations, and many principles have been discovered and articulated. While some are redundant, obsolete, or overly specific, there is great value in having multiple frameworks, just as there is value in understanding multiple languages. Researching across many disciplines can reveal deep principles not otherwise visible, and having multiple tools at your fingertips affords flexibility in dealing with situations. The most effective use of frameworks comes when the frameworks are aligned to complement each other: each addresses different aspects of a situation, without overlap or contradictions.

9

Building Trust through Giving Relationships

Understanding and Developing Extraverted Feeling

Benefits for Self-Leadership

As you develop extraverted Feeling, you will
- Improve networking skills and work relationships
- Be more responsive to people's feelings, values, preferences, needs, and opinions
- Bring people closer together around shared needs and values
- Deepen trust for more meaningful relationships

Assessing Current Development

Before continuing, check the phrases in the table that describe you well.

Part 1
☐ Easily discern other people's needs, preferences, and values.
☐ Feel inclined to be responsible for and take care of others' feelings.
☐ Help people feel comfortable by engaging in hosting and care-taking.

Part 2
☐ Recognize and adhere to shared values, feelings, and social norms to get along.
☐ Merge and feel intimate oneness with other people.

Part 3
☐ Reciprocate appreciation and honor the support others give you.
☐ Easily take on someone else's needs and values as your own.
☐ Easily communicate personally to all members of a group to feel unity.

Scoring: Assign one point to items in part 1, two points to items in part 2, and three points to items in part 3.

Total points: 7

A score above nine indicates a likely preference for extraverted Feeling. A score from four to nine indicates a possible supporting preference or development from life experience. A score below four suggests a lack of development.

Understanding How Extraverted Feeling Works

At the core of extraverted Feeling is a giving relationship. This might be the empathic connectedness of a husband and wife of many years who've stood by each other, or the sincere and heartfelt desire to help a stranger. Sometimes all we need is to say something kind and offer something of value to demonstrate our intentions. By giving, we show trust and invite the other person to reciprocate. Other times a history of genuine empathy is needed since it is not quite enough to act nicely only when you must rely on a person in times of true hardship.

Best-Use Activities

What can we do in a giving relationship? We can ask for help and place trust in the other person. Because of the experiences, values, feelings, and responsibilities we've shared before now, the other person knows us and can give us helpful advice. We might ask someone to protect us or retrieve something for us, feeling that we can rely on that person. Or we can ask for and give honesty. When we feel encouraged and have each other's best interests at heart, we reap the fruit of giving, which is strong relationships, partnerships, and alliances.

Support includes asking for aid in dealing with third parties. We can ask those close to us to take our side on an issue not because of rational agreement but because we are calling on the promise of social and intimate bonds. We can call on each other, keeping in mind all we've done before. We may be disappointed if the other person doesn't reciprocate, but our feelings often encourage us to try again.

To decide what others need as individuals or as a group, we can observe how people interact with each other. This involves focusing on people's feelings, values, and interests and attending to the social networks around us. Without this awareness we might end up imposing on people while expecting something nice in return, or we might expect something they can't give us.

We believe that a community comes together through shared values and mutual support and that cultural norms are aids to getting off on the right foot and staying there. We might even show great kindness to strangers and even those opposing us since we might need each other in the future. Mentoring is a gift to help earn the respect of future generations and the respect of the larger group.

Choosing safe relationships and creating safe "spaces" for our relationships is crucial. With everyone we care to get close to or at least not offend, we consider how a word or gesture will be taken or what people will relate to. If we offend, then what can we expect in return? We take seriously the opinions of the people we respect and

FIG. 9.1. Cognitive snapshot of extraverted feeling

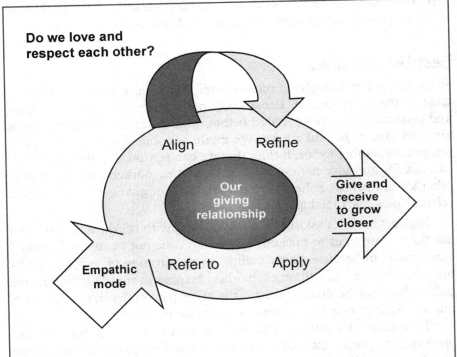

Do we love and respect each other?

Align

Refine

Our giving relationship

Give and receive to grow closer

Empathic mode

Refer to

Apply

At the core of extraverted Feeling is a giving relationship with someone else. When we go into an empathic mode, we focus on others' needs and take on their needs and values as our own. We can refer to, align, refine, and apply a relationship. Applying often means giving and receiving support to grow closer. We reflect on our giving relationship by asking, do we both love, trust, and respect each other?

value, just as we hope they listen to us in return. Since mistakes will be made, we may forgive when a promise is broken. All we say and do can be viewed in the context of our relationships. We might wonder whether an inappropriate request or gift was offered deliberately. Are we being treated with respect? Can we negotiate a better relationship? We should offer an apology if we hurt someone, but what if that person uses it against us? Will people change their behavior if we change ours first?

Some relationships get special attention. Touching starts a physiological process that greatly strengthens bonds. Romance is a heightened exchange leading toward union. Sharing our feelings, weaknesses, and fears is an intimate way to nurture a deep relationship. We might even take on someone's needs and values as our own. We might keep our desk tidy to please a respected boss, move to another city so a spouse can pursue a job opportunity, or take up a hobby to spend more time with friends.

People who prefer extraverted Feeling draw on personal interactions and socially relevant roles to maintain a feeling of caring and support as they navigate life and make sense of all aspects of living.

Mind-Set and Feedback

Using extraverted Feeling requires that we be personal, compassionate, and without hard boundaries. We may wonder how to aid someone we care for, which needs and values someone might consider to better himself or herself, or if his or her associates are exerting a positive influence. Do we know when and how to leave an unpleasant relationship? Will certain words and actions ensure goodwill, encourage fair offers, and help others' relationships? What comes around goes around: word gets out and our reputation is enhanced or compromised based on our choices. The better our people-reading and social-networking skills, the more likely we are to detect who is improved or trustworthy and how to support those close to us.

We can evaluate our relationships by looking at the balance of giving and receiving. When there is mutual love, trust, and respect, we have a tremendous feeling of joy.

Possible Misuses

Sometimes use of the extraverted Feeling process becomes rigid and dominating because of stress or because it is used without skill and without other processes to balance it. When this occurs, we may

- Find we have to keep voicing values and opinions because people aren't responding in kind
- Be perceived by others as helping too much and perhaps forgetting people's uncommunicated boundaries
- Find ourselves having to rely on interpersonal conflict to build or maintain a relationship
- Try to use community norms or group power to force others to adopt our values
- Feel dependent on other people (rather than interdependent) and perhaps overly influenced by their words, feelings, and actions

Case Studies

The following vignettes illustrate extraverted Feeling. The first is an everyday situation and the second includes use with other processes in an organizational setting.

Case A

Diana is concerned about a new supervisor at work. He isn't very social, which makes it difficult to relate to him, and Diana wonders if he is aware of others' feelings when he comments on their work. She considers if everyone got off on the wrong foot and asks around if anyone said something offensive. They'd skipped the usual get-to-  know-you office party because of the tight budget. That let down people. A few weeks later the situation improved slightly. Diana had arranged for some nice amenities for the supervisor's office, but apparently he wasn't using them. She felt hurt but then asked him about it. It turned out he hadn't noticed them. Fortunately, the relationship now allows her to ask whether there's been a problem. He explains that he is very allergic to others' perfume but didn't want to say anything and create a problem. Diana sighs: now she has to deal with half the office.

Case B

Saul, a senator, has given many years to helping his constituents. Most of his concern
involves negotiating with other elected officials,
networking with lobbyists, and enjoying the
company of his extended family. He values a
personal touch and remains connected to the
people he grew up with. With every bill, getting

people to cooperate can be difficult. Clear communication helps. He's
known as very friendly and fair and is often called upon to mediate. He
tries his best to recognize every side of an issue, ensuring that everyone's
opinion is heard and that everyone is respectful of each other's values.
Sometimes he feels that he gives a lot for the little he gets in return. But
the thoughtful gifts and thank-you letters from constituents keep him
feeling needed.

Perspective Shifting

Here are some suggestions for how to communicate with, learn from,
and influence someone who is using extraverted Feeling.

- **Communicating to Build Rapport**
  - Ask and show appreciation for how the other person is giving
    in his or her relationships. The person may refer to roles such
    as a parent or employee or, more likely, to specific people by
    name. We can give and help each other in many ways. Use
    this person's terms when you converse.
  - To gauge how the person feels about these relationships, ask
    whether this person feels appreciated, loved, or respected
    (as appropriate). Is this person getting back what he or she
    deserves? Show empathy. Make a few offers to show kind-
    ness, and nod in sympathy or show concern when the person
    describes the relationshis' ups and downs.

- **Learning to Build New Skills**
  - Ask what exactly the person tends to give and likes to receive.
    Ask the person to describe these for you in terms of gifts,
    praise, help with problems, inclusion in activities, mentoring
    and advice, role modeling, and shared values.

- Ask the person to describe his or her giving and receiving process. What specific cues suggest others' needs? How much does this person check by asking? Who else is involved? How are each person's values different? How does this person want to be appreciated? After an exchange, what tells the person that it has been positive and sincere?

- **Influencing for Best Use**
  - How well are these interactions creating lasting bonds? What has this person not received from someone? How has this person communicated needs? What have others been giving instead?
  - Ask how often the person has gone into an empathic mode. That is, how much time has this person devoted to meeting others' feelings and needs, and stepping into their shoes? Who is this person avoiding?

- **Helping to Discover New Outcomes**
  - How much has the giving relationship created a feeling of love or joy or a sense of community?
  - If the person is dissatisfied, could he or she engage in a giving relationship with another person? (The person may not know what that new relationship might be.)

Everything can be considered in terms of how it affects other people.

Developing Extraverted Feeling

The following exercises will help you develop the extraverted Feeling process. Get your self-assessment score from the beginning of this chapter and then set your starting point using the chart below.

If you scored	Then start with
0–3	The Introductory Exercises
4–9	The Basic Exercises
10+	The Advanced Exercises

As you work through the coming exercises, you may find some are particularly challenging. Include all the following steps to get more satisfying use of this process:

1. To access the process in the most effective way, go into a sincere empathic mode. (See pages 166–167 to enter this mode.)

2. Access the core of the process: decide whom to give to and receive from to nurture a relationship.

3. Engage in best-use activities, such as expressing your needs and preferences and asking about the needs, values, and exchanges in your social network.

4. Try for a desired outcome by making an offer or evaluating what's received. Do you feel you're growing closer?

5. Get feedback and calibrate: are we united in a loving, supportive, and respectful relationship with each other?

6. Integrate your use of extraverted Feeling with other cognitive processes (usually introverted Sensing or introverted Intuiting).

As you develop this process, you'll be able to engage these steps all at once for increasingly coordinated and smooth use.

Introductory Exercises

These exercises will help you get comfortable giving and receiving as you build supportive, empathic, and intimate relationships with others.

FIND SOMEONE IN NEED

Do something nice for someone for no reason other than to be nice. Choose someone who's been working a lot or has been ill or lonely or is otherwise in need of encouragement. This person might be a loved one or an acquaintance. Don't think about what you might get in return since this exercise is about giving for its own sake. Just consider what it is like to be that person and how it would feel to receive a gift.

PICK OUT A GIFT

Something that is a mild surprise is a nice gift, such as making the person dinner or fixing something he or she hasn't had time or money to repair. Ask the person's friends and loved ones for guidance. Your gift should be something that shows you care about this person, something he or she both likes and needs. (Not everything we like is necessary, and not everything we need is liked.) Remember, the most precious gifts aren't valued in dollars; they show that we know the recipient and they offer something money can't really buy, like love, free time, or a few moments of peace of mind. Remember The Platinum Rule®: Give unto others what they want to receive.

ACCEPT THE REACTION

When you give the gift—preferably in person—also give a moment for the recipient to discover and enjoy it, then join with him or her. Notice the person's reaction and allow yourself to feel what this person feels. Open yourself to receiving the happiness and gratitude as if they were your own. (It will likely be a pleasing gift because you researched it.) Consider that what we give to each other we give to ourselves.

Basic Exercises

These exercises will help you become comfortable getting to know people, from finding out others' needs and values to communicating honestly and being alert to unhealthy behavior.

GET TO KNOW MANY PEOPLE

It's easier to create relationships with others when we know them as individuals, and people are most willing to share themselves when we demonstrate a willingness to share too. As you get to know people, talk about yourself as you find out about their lives. Engage in exchange. Ask about their career, background, interests, and family to discover their values. The more deeply you know people, the easier it will be to figure out their values and needs.

UNDERSTAND OTHERS THROUGH KNOWLEDGE

One way to read people is to rationally consider, what if you were them? Think how you might respond considering other people's situations, past experiences, current relationships, and needs and values. Sometimes one detail about them can make a huge difference in your understanding, so stay tuned in and leave room to discover new information, especially if their behavior seems off. Also remember that most people don't behave unemotionally. For example, if someone seriously wronged them in the past, they may have forgiven the person or they may hold a grudge, but they are unlikely to simply not care.

KNOW OTHERS AS THEY ARE

Another way to increase your understanding is to focus on others, stepping into their shoes and getting a feel for them. Watch others discreetly. Imagine standing where they are standing and doing, seeing, and hearing from their perspective. For example, watch a mother in the market with her children. Stand close to where she's standing. Try on her facial expressions and posture. Listen to what she's hearing. After a few moments, you will begin to feel as she does. You might feel exasperation, love, concern, and many other emotions mixed together. Remember as you do this exercise that it isn't necessarily your responsibility to help the person.

PURSUE THE HARD CASES

Reading other people's needs, values, thoughts, and feelings isn't always easy. Some people are rather closed. They may find it hard to start a conversation, much less a relationship. Perhaps they are hesitant because of past bad experiences. Or maybe they do not share the same interests most people do. Remember to honor all people for who they are, even when you feel they could benefit from stronger relationships. Just let them know you are available if needed, and check regularly that everything is okay.

DETERMINE YOUR NEEDS AND VALUES

Knowing your needs and values also helps you understand others. Consider and, if possible, prioritize your needs and values. What do you really need emotionally, physically, financially, and so on? Also consider what you don't need and already have in abundance—this is what you value. For example, if you are poor to the point of being unable to properly give to your family yet you have many good friends and neighbors who like you, then perhaps you need money and value positive relationships. Consider ways your life differs from others' and thus how your needs and values likely differ from theirs.

LOCATE SHARED VALUES AND COMMON SOLUTIONS

Consider the people you are with and the values they all share. For example, even when your friends come from different political parties they likely share a sense of national pride. And businesses likely share values around success in general, whether that means profit, personal advancement, or contributions to the world. When faced with problems, encourage others to share these common values and support solutions that meet everyone's values.

CREATE SAFE SPACES FOR HONEST COMMUNICATION

When you experience a problem with someone else, first find a comfortable environment to share your concerns with him or her and be sure the relationship is presently safe enough to continue. You can check safety by asking others who know the person, checking whether that person's behavior matches statements made, and noting influence from third parties. If and when you feel ready, you can take a risk making your feelings known and invite the other person to reciprocate. People communicate in many ways. They may be direct or indirect. Sometimes people aren't sure what they value or need, and they may say so and ask for more time, personal space, or assistance in identifying what they need. Communication is an ongoing process that requires care because once words are said they cannot be taken back.

CHOOSE HEALTHY RELATIONSHIPS

Choose friends and potential loved ones wisely. When you self-disclose, does the other person reciprocate? When discussing a problem to resolve, does the other person admit his or her fair share and stay clear of starting an argument? Beware of bullies—people who deliberately make offers you don't want and then become angry at your response. Similarly, beware of people who repeatedly ask for help and then complain it's not good enough or they don't like it. Drama that is created early on for its own sake signals something may be wrong. You will know a relationship is positive when each person in the relationship feels truly open to and supportive of each other, facing matters together with trust.

Advanced Exercises

These exercises will help you hone your basic use of the extraverted Feeling process and develop some advanced use. Learn to take a more active role in social networking and listening to others' advice.

ATTEND TO A NETWORK OF RELATIONSHIPS

When you get involved with someone else, you are likely getting involved with everyone he or she knows, so consider not only a person's relationship with you but that person's relationships with others as well—his or her parents, friends, colleagues, children, neighbors, pets, and so on. Pay a lot of attention to each person's interactions with others. This involves noticing who pays attention to whom and when, the offers people make and what they are willing to receive, and so on.

BETTER KNOW OTHERS FROM THEIR INTERACTIONS

You can learn a lot about people from looking at their friends, how they treat others, and what they say about others to you. Someone who gossips to you about others may be likely to gossip about you. Someone mean to others may become mean to you. Or you may notice that someone needs help with a relationship or is being highly influenced by or is obliged to another person—someone is doing what another person wants without getting much if anything in return. Whom do people spend time with? Where do they get their values? If they are doing poorly or well in a relationship with someone, who is encouraging or discouraging them? A bad influence on them can affect you and all your relationships negatively as well.

SUPPORT WITH GENUINE AFFIRMATION

When someone is doing poorly or going through a bad time, lend support. This can be practical. Be sure to give plenty of genuine praise and affirmations. Genuine praise reminds the person of what he or she is truly good at and expresses that you know too. Disingenuous praise sets the person up for trying to succeed at something he or she is not good at or feeling guilty if he or she doesn't fulfill expectations. Genuine praise relieves pressure and worry about what will occur if success doesn't happen or if the person is not ready to be fully on his or her own yet.

LISTEN TO OTHERS' ADVICE

When you need help or are having a bad day, look to others for positive support. Be open to advice from those who know you and your needs and values and have your interests at heart. Sometimes you may not like the advice. What we need for our future happiness isn't always something we want to hear. Teenagers often don't like to hear they should study hard, yet parents know studying will provide many future benefits and more happiness.

GET IN TOUCH WITH SOCIETY'S VALUES

We are not alone, and each of our lives, while unique, is not unlike others'. It is helpful to separate our individual needs and values from society's messages to us about what's valuable. It is also helpful to consider how others have succeeded in getting their needs met. Consider the institutions and paths society provides to help us get our needs met and which of those match best with others' values.

MAINTAIN INTERDEPENDENT RELATIONSHIPS

When we open up and give a lot of ourselves, we may be taken advantage of or feel hurt by others' missteps, such as using poorly chosen words. Increase interdependence to maintain relationships. To help reset a relationship on a positive path, help both parties discuss together past mistakes and ways to improve the relationship in the future. First, create a safe space, such as mutually agreed-upon ground rules for interaction. The focus is the relationship or community, not just each person as an individual. Airing grievances diplomatically can relieve negative emotions and surface issues, but this process isn't about blame; it's about regaining trust by reconnecting and joining together to address what's happening. The parties should make a promise to each other and fulfill it as a gesture of good faith. Watch for possible unhealthy behavior—selfishness, negativity, divisive ideas, or lying. Such behavior can be dealt with through social pressure—by increasing the number and strength of relationships around the two people.

NURTURE SUPPORTIVE FRIENDSHIPS

Nurture group support. The more, the better. Make sure you are there for your friends when they go through their trials and they are more likely to be there for you. (A friend in need is a friend indeed!) The support can be moral support, or it can be an authority figure or the weight of the community, the justice system, or a shared circle of friends. Having people who can act as boundaries and intermediaries can be invaluable.

SURROUND YOURSELF WITH COMMUNITY

The more you surround yourself with lots of positive people who care about you, the less unethical and selfish people will matter or affect you. Look to family or a community where you are welcomed, respected, and loved. Wherever shared needs and values are present, people naturally come together in mutual support.

BE AN ADMIRABLE ROLE MODEL

One way to discourage selfishness is through good examples and positive role models worthy of respect and admiration. Honor your agreements with and promises to others, be forgiving but not foolish, and look for ways to bring people together through their commonalities. Everyone is human and has human needs—food, shelter, company, and work that is fulfilling and meaningful. By considering each other's individual needs as valuable—and by giving unconditional respect regardless of background, present circumstances, education, or ethnicity—you can speak to all people at once. This is compassion.

MERGE WITH OTHERS

Merging with someone else is the greatest gift two people can give each other. Merging means taking on someone else's commitments and values as our own, opening ourselves up to truly take on what the other person feels. We put such trust in the person that we cease to worry or question. And this merging is not limited to one person. Our families, our community, the entire human race—these become ours and we become theirs.

10

Staying True to
Who You Really Are

Understanding and Developing Introverted Feeling

Benefits for Self-Leadership

As you develop introverted Feeling, you will
- Evoke loyalty and commitment to larger issues and goals
- Make choices that harmonize with what's truly important in life
- Know what you want personally and how to motivate yourself
- Be more in touch with your and others' beliefs and what's important

Assessing Current Development

Before continuing, check the phrases in the table that describe you well.

Part 1
☐ Feel strongly that something is good or bad.
☐ Keep listening to your conscience when making daily choices.
☐ Remain true to what you want for yourself or others.

Part 2
☐ Identify and defend what someone truly wants.
☐ Continually evaluate what is worth believing in and most important to you personally.

Part 3
☐ Remain in touch with what you want, what motivates you, and what is good.
☐ Create space within yourself for the truth of conflicting beliefs.
☐ Continually weigh whether choices harmonize with important beliefs.

Scoring: Assign one point to items in part 1, two points to items in part 2, and three points to items in part 3.

Total points:

A score above nine indicates a likely preference for introverted Feeling. A score from four to nine indicates a possible supporting preference or development from life experience. A score below four suggests a lack of development.

Understanding How Introverted Feeling Works

At the core of introverted Feeling are the deep personal convictions that makes us who we are. Our identity is who we are down deep to our bones. We are the sum of our choices and commitments, culture and relationships, attitudes and beliefs, life path, and humanity. Identity can include our group or the link we have to all creatures by virtue of being alive. Identity is how we are ourselves in the most individual and partial ways, even when our beliefs are about the most universal qualities of human existence.

Best-Use Activities

What can we do with a personal identity? We can explore, reflect on, and reconsider who we really are. What motivates us? What do we want for ourselves and others? We might ask if a choice or situation is congruent with our identity, what's worth believing in, and whether others believe in us. We stay in touch with what we want, what moves us, and how we feel inside. Our convictions might be just for us or for an organization. Often these aren't issues we need to puzzle over when we are in touch with who we are.

We can ask about others' identities and compare them to our own and to the people, groups, causes, ideas, and places we are loyal to. This might involve listening, dialoging, and observing behavior to get a better feel for someone's character. Is this person being authentic? We feel simpatico with those who share our identity and loyal to those who are authentic. Our silent empathy with all living things tends to attract people. They sense a "vibe" or body language suggesting that we relate to them. We may not, and sometimes this attracts the worst sorts of people longing for help. Whom can we trust not to betray our beliefs? Who accepts and respects us for who we are? To what extent is something good or bad? Should we take on a particular cause or fight an injustice? Do we choose to let others live true to themselves, even when their identities contradict our values or even threaten human life? What is most important for the institutions and organizations around us?

Each of our choices becomes a part of our identity and subject to the pains of our conscience. A choice may sully us or express our deepest values or both: we continually examine choices to see whether they match our inner value systems and intent, even as we recognize that the ironic contradictions of human nature are inescapable. We may wonder if something is above or beneath who we believe we are. It's important to live our lives and run our organizations in congruence with our beliefs, for perhaps if we don't, we are hypocrites. With a major choice, we may dwell a long time on careful consideration before devoting ourselves, exploring how we can live with ourselves if we internalize a new set of values. Once we choose, we will stay true to what we want for ourselves and others.

FIG. 10.1. Cognitive snapshot of introverted feeling

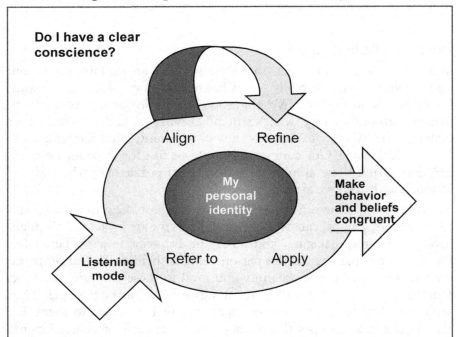

At the core of introverted Feeling is one's personal identity, the sum of individual choices, beliefs, and attitudes. When we go into a listening mode, we pay careful attention to our conscience and others' feedback. We can refer to, align, refine, and apply our personal identity. Applying often means making our behavior congruent with our beliefs. We reflect on our personal identity by asking, do I have a clear conscience?

We can use this process to evoke what's important to others. What words, policies, images, and actions fit people's self-conceptions? For example, we might determine that a new strategy won't be truly accepted by a team, or a new brand accepted by the public, unless it can be aligned to their beliefs and self-image. We can also disrupt assumptions, confront issues, and spark universal appeal. A painter might use key images to provoke people's deepest beliefs and hold them up for reflection.

Identity is mostly silent and indefinable, a great ocean; the surface waters break only when a deep personal value is violated. When we witness others' suffering wrought by evil, we can experience great pathos and desire to defend them. Sometimes a single value dominates and we feel strongly that something is simply good or bad. Then the expression of our identity may no longer be our own but a reaction to someone else's. At our best, we might identify and defend what another person truly wants, regardless of our own values, so long as that desire does not harm others. They have their own choices to make. For society and the organizations we are a part of, using this process helps us stay centered on what's important for success even as we stay true to ethical and just aspirations. Identity is a gift that can make everything worthwhile.

Those who prefer introverted Feeling rely on their personal identity—their innermost values, attitudes, and beliefs—to navigate life and make sense of all aspects of living.

Mind-Set and Feedback

Using introverted Feeling requires that we be subjective and personal, to be honest to ourselves—always true and listening to our beliefs, what's important to us, and our conscience. To be who we are, we must willingly strip away all that is manufactured and trite to stay tuned in to the center of ourselves. Ideally, our identity demands that we continually weigh the relative value or worth of everything, considering the intrinsic value and remembering we are unique and not alone.

Our conscience helps us understand the result of staying true to our root beliefs, and listening to it may lead to reconsideration and new choices. When our conscience is satisfied, we have a tremendous feeling of harmonious balance.

Possible Misuses

Sometimes use of the introverted Feeling process becomes rigid and dominating because of stress or because it is used without skill and without other processes to balance it. When this occurs, we may

- Be forgetful about having heard or seen something because it doesn't our match beliefs
- Allow people space to choose what they want, then feel somewhat angry and mistreated later
- Find we have stopped listening as we have stuck so closely or "purely" with a conviction that we have blocked personal growth and natural change
- React to an injustice in an all-or-nothing way without being open to negotiation or to seeing from another perspective
- Find ourselves crusading for a belief, demanding that others adhere to it, even when this attitude may be causing harm

Case Studies

The following vignettes illustrate introverted Feeling. The first is an everyday situation and the second includes use with other processes in an organizational setting.

Case A

Kurt overheard a father scolding his young son for jumping on the park benches. Kurt often came to the park to relax. The trees don't have issues, he reflected. He was struck by the irony that inner peace might come at the price of not being human. Kids deserve to be kids, he thought, and everyone deserves to be themselves. What harm is the boy doing? Kurt wanted to ask. But he wasn't one to push his beliefs. He  opened his guitar case and began playing. The kid stopped jumping and ran over. "Don't bother the man, Tim," the dad called. "Can I play?" the kid asked excitedly. "It's fine," Kurt said to the dad, then, smiling, offered to show the boy how to play a chord. This was just his thing. He hoped the father and son would grow closer after today. Using his profits over the years, Kurt sponsored a nonprofit music camp to help troubled children.

Case B

Patty is a art psychologist. A close friend once remarked to her that she took clients to the "center of themselves." This sounded so right to Patty, and from that day she began listening to colleagues' responses as she shared her techniques at conferences. Then someone said something that shook her. This person, Patty

thought, is misusing my words to halt self-reflection and growth, by intellectualizing this. When someone casually asked her about it, she expressed her concerns. Sympathetic colleagues then launched a training program. She also began statistical research after a respected mentor asked about the validity of her ideas. Now, after seventeen years, a very successful nationwide organization has sprung up around her—people following her ideas, getting together, and spreading the word.

Perspective Shifting

Here are some suggestions for how to communicate with, learn from, and influence someone who is using introverted Feeling.

- **Communicating to Build Rapport**
  - Ask the other person about his or her personal convictions. The person may refer to identity, beliefs, values, commitments, attitudes, choices, group affiliation, religion, morals and ethics, humanity, existence, or roles they fulfill in life. Use this person's terms when you converse.
  - To gauge how the person feels about himself or herself at the moment, ask how he or she feels about his or her life right now. Then ask how this person feels about these feelings. Refrain from judging or defining. To get past impersonal or grand statements, such as references to all humanity, cultural roles, or personality type, ask questions about choices and commitments this person has made.

- **Learning to Build New Skills**
  - Ask what about living life is important to the person, and what has worth relative to other values, actions, and so on.

Ask the person to describe for you the choices and commitments he or she has made and continues to remake every single day.

- Ask the person how his or her attitudes and beliefs are formed. How much is by direct experience and how much is by hypothesizing? What moments in situations personally move this person the most? What does this person tend to consider most when clarifying or discarding a belief? How does he or she experience listening to his or her conscience?

- **Influencing for Best Use**
  - How well do various aspects of this person "live together"? Ask the person to describe contradictory choices and beliefs.
  - Ask how much this person has been able to go into a listening mode and what aspects of life he or she may be shutting out or not hearing because they don't fit with who this person believes he or she is.

- **Helping to Discover New Outcomes**
  - Is this person's conscience satisfied? Do beliefs help the person get to the core of who he or she is? You may need to give examples from your own or others' lives.
  - If the person is dissatisfied, would another personal identity and set of beliefs meet with the approval of his or her conscience? (The person may not know what this new identity might be.)

Everything can be brought into harmony or congruence if you truly believe it can be.

Developing Introverted Feeling

These exercises will help you develop this process. Get your self-assessment score from the beginning of the chapter and then set your starting point using the chart below.

If you scored	Then start with
0–3	The Introductory Exercises
4–9	The Basic Exercises
10+	The Advanced Exercises

As you work through the coming exercises, you may find some are particularly challenging. Include all the following steps to get more satisfying use of this process:

1. To access the process in the most effective way, go into a reflective listening mode. (See pages 166–167 to enter this mode.)

2. Access the core of the process: what is your personal identity or identities? This is the sum of your beliefs, choices, and commitments.

3. Engage in best-use activities, such as evaluating what is important and worth standing up for or considering what impact a choice of commitment will have on who you are.

4. Try for a desired outcome by living out who you are—making your behavior congruent with your beliefs.

5. Get feedback and calibrate: what does your conscience tell you? Does what you are considering feel "good"?

6. Integrate your use of introverted Feeling with other cognitive processes (usually extraverted Sensing or extraverted Intuiting).

As you develop this process, you'll be able to engage these steps all at once for increasingly coordinated and smooth use.

Introductory Exercises

These exercises will help you get comfortable observing and dealing with situations according to your conscience as you make choices and commitments every day.

GET REACQUAINTED WITH YOURSELF

Identify how you feel right now. How do you feel about how you feel? Perhaps you're sad at the moment but happy overall. Also, identify what you believe. Perhaps select something that is important to you today. What do you believe about what you believe?

EVALUATE YOUR VALUES AND LIFE FOR CONGRUENCY

Examine all aspects of your life for congruence between your daily choices and your beliefs. Walk through one day in which at each step you listen to your conscience, asking yourself, how well does this agree with my beliefs?

IMPLEMENT A SMALL CHANGE

Resolve to make a small change—one you truly value and want to do to live out something you believe. You might start recycling, set aside more time with family, take a more energy-efficient way to work, or change your diet. Listen to your conscience when you encounter pressure against keeping your resolution. Your conscience will help guide you to stick with what's truly important.

Basic Exercises

These exercises will help you get comfortable exploring your personal identity, from exploring where your values come from to facing limiting beliefs, unintended consequences, and conflicting commitments.

GET IN TOUCH WITH WANTS AND MOTIVATIONS

What do you really want? What motivates you? You can begin to answer by paying attention to what energizes you. When a student attends classes with lackluster enthusiasm, then perhaps it is the wrong major for her, or perhaps college is not the best path for him. Consider what brings you personal happiness. This is not about selfishness, it is about making sure we take care of ourselves and are engaging our natural gifts and talents.

REVIEW YOUR LIFE CHOICES

Review the choices you've made through your life—from big, one-time choices to small choices you are remaking every day. For example, if you've stopped speaking to someone or you've started selling a product, consider how that is a choice you remake every day. How much energy and impact is that choice causing?

REEVALUATE UNINTENDED CONSEQUENCES

Look at some unintended consequences of your choices over the years. What did you do when you saw the consequences: apologize? Try to right things? Continue on? How you followed up was a choice. How do you feel as you reflect on these times? Assume that everything that happens is important in some way, that it increases understanding, can be viewed as a test, or improves life directly for someone. What did you and others gain and what did you lose? Consider what other people you know have done in the same situation. Was your choice a typical human reaction? Consider how you or your organization could follow up again with greater satisfaction or respond differently in the future to a similar situation.

ATTEND TO OTHERS' VALUES

In a group of people, offer a comment and watch how others react; see what brings a smile, energy, or fear, anger, or another strong emotion. These reactions suggest what's important to these people, even if what's important isn't being voiced. Consider what values lie behind their words or reactions. Look for examples of hypocrisy in daily life. Now look at yourself. ("Judge not, lest you be judged!") How would you judge yourself in light of your own and others' values?

EXPLORE WHERE YOUR VALUES AND BELIEFS COME FROM

Consider where your beliefs and attitudes come from: your culture, parents, colleagues, and peers or your organization. Which beliefs apply to you personally, and which could you continue your life without? Consider which beliefs are reactions against your culture, family, or friends.

PUT ASIDE LIMITING BELIEFS

Consider beliefs that affect your daily life. If you have an opinion or belief that doesn't truly apply to you, then if you let go of the belief, would anything change (except maybe you)? Also consider if you might be holding such beliefs to limit others around you in some way, which also limits yourself. That is not an easy question and may take some time to answer. Talking to a friend may help. When might you be ready to let go of these beliefs?

HONOR CONFLICTING FEELINGS

Try as often as you can during the day, when faced with a choice large or small, to listen to your conscience. Consider how you feel in that moment: happy, ashamed, conflicted, thankful, at peace, angry? Allow that emotion to well up and express itself inside you. You don't need to act on it or talk about it. Just allow yourself to experience it. This can be difficult if you are in a position of responsibility, such as a manager or leader, and have to balance the worth of various actions and people's values.

WEIGH DEGREES OF IMPORTANCE

Make a list of everything you tend to say and do. You might want to solicit feedback from others. Read your list aloud. Now add the word "always," as in "I always go to work on time." How important is the action that you always do it? If "always" doesn't feel right, then consider any underlying beliefs. What mitigates your action? Now make a list of things you don't do and say and read it aloud, adding the word "never." Reflect again in the same way.

EXPLORE YOUR RANGE OF CHOICES

Think of a recent situation where you were uncomfortable or had to make a choice quickly. What was the feeling in that moment? How did you feel about that? And how do you feel now? Did you want to leave, stay, help, or say something? Upon reflection, list all the choices you could have made. Then imagine yourself in a similar situation in the future. Try out each choice to gauge your conscience before, during, and after making it.

EXPLORE YOUR VALUES IN DEPTH

Write a song, poem, or story to explore what's important to you personally. This exercise is just for you. Listen to your conscience as you compose and ask if you're expressing yourself in a true way.

Advanced Exercises

These exercises will help you hone your basic use of the introverted Feeling process and develop some advanced use. Learn to take a more active role in creating and maintaining your personal identity.

ACTIVELY LISTEN TO OTHERS

Listen to the people around you. Just listen. Focus on tone of voice and overall energy level. Consider what's motivating each person. What is genuine or sounds as though people are trying to convince or deceive themselves, or what comes across as acting? Are people's words aligned with their behavior? What do they say? If you suspect a particular underlying value or belief, ask a question. A good question directs a person to look deeper within; he or she may not respond immediately, so allow time. Or try repeating back what the person said and listen for his or her response. Are there certain key words or ideas that people easily get excited about? These reactions indicate values.

RECONCILE CONFLICTING VALUES

By now you may have come across some contradictory values, such as wanting free time with your family members but also wanting to earn enough money to make sure they are secure. Acting in accord with both can be challenging. List people you know who are in similar situations and consider how they handle the contradiction. Listen for what their beliefs are.

EXAMINE YOUR MORAL COMPROMISES

Consider moral compromises you have made over the years—that is, deliberate choices that bothered your conscience but felt necessary either for a greater good, the good of another, or your own good. This isn't about failings or guilt. This exercise explores how you go about living in a complex world.

RESEARCH OTHERS' BELIEF SYSTEMS

Volunteer to help the less fortunate, perhaps people who are less successful or less happy. What do their words and deeds say about their values and beliefs? Are their words congruent with their values or are some of these people kidding themselves? Now spend time with people more fortunate.

Listen for their beliefs. Are their words congruent or are some of these people kidding themselves? Compare similarities and differences. Who is alone or happier?

BE ALL-INCLUSIVE

Consider what beliefs allow for all these belief systems, each having its own worth or "goodness." What beliefs could allow for all of these to exist peaceably at once?

EXPLORE OTHERS' TRUTHS

What if you adopted some of these other beliefs? Write a song, poem, or short story reflecting a different belief from the first-person point of view. As you compose, allow yourself free expression of who you would be with a dedication to what actually would happen, not what you think should happen. For example, you might write about yourself as a thief who gets away with a crime; although you "should" be caught by the police, maybe you escape. What does this mean? How do you choose to live in a world where this is possible? When you are done, write a second piece reflecting a different belief.

CONSIDER ALTERNATIVE FEELINGS AND BELIEFS

Consider a problem situation in your life, ways you'd like it to be, and choices you can make. List as many choices as you can, even ones that you wouldn't normally make or that go against your beliefs, just for the sake of the list. Consider how you feel about the situation and different ways you might feel with each choice. Generally we hear that we cannot help how we feel, or we hear that others cause us to feel certain ways. (But how can they physically cause this?) But this feeling is for you. Now consider which beliefs and feelings will get you the best result from the situation.

REFLECT ON WHAT'S IMPORTANT TO SAY

For a day, before speaking, consider how your words express a belief. If you're unsure, mentally explore by asking, when is this true? And according to whom for whom? Consider ways to reword your responses so you're not pushing yourself onto others.

EVALUATE OTHERS' IMPACT ON YOU

Listen extra carefully to those who know you and the people you work for. Who believes in you? What tells you they believe in you? What are their values and how well do these align with who you are? Are you comfortable with the actions of the organizations and institutions you're in? Consider that always allowing others what they want can be harmful, and even when people mean well they can be less than helpful. Who is truly important and of value to you, regardless of circumstances? Explore how you know this.

REVISIT THE CENTER OF YOURSELF

Review all your values and beliefs. Now mentally strip away some. As you strip away each one, ask, "Who am I?" "How might my life be different without this belief?" Mentally strip away as many of your beliefs as possible. Now who are you? Consider that you are the sum of your choices, past and current. Consider everything you can do and who you can be with freedom from yourself.

EXPLORE THE NATURE OF EVIL

What do you believe is evil? Start with examples from firsthand experience. How did you decide malevolence was present? Now, in contrast, imagine someone who does only good every day as part of living his or her life. What if this someone were you? How would you, your life, and the people around you be different? Now imagine making a deliberate choice that causes harm. Imagine someone who does this every day. Reflect on why you believe evil exists.

ALLOW PEOPLE THEIR CHOICES

Consider which choices are yours and which choices are for others to make. If you have a value about how people should treat the environment and others don't seem to be listening or following through, then at what point do you allow others to experience the consequences of their choices? Where do you find peace? Consider ways to move a situation toward maximum goodness for each individual without imposing your personal beliefs or causing harm to others or to yourself.

MERGE WITH WHO YOU ARE

Merge with your beliefs at every moment. Consider everything you've learned above, centering yourself in who you are; balancing the relative importance of various people, ideas, and options; and making choices while listening to and following your conscience. The result is true peace of mind and living by example.

11

From Awareness to Action

Boosting Energy and Shifting Perspectives to Maximize Development

Putting Knowledge into Practice

Unlike the sage's suggestion above, you probably want to begin the self-leadership process right away. This is not always easy, and people often have numerous questions: How do we know if we're focusing too much on one process? Is there a general exercise to catalyze learning? Are there pitfalls to keep in mind? How can we get more comfortable engaging a particular

process? These kinds of questions are natural. You will learn answers to these questions and more. In this chapter you will learn how to
- Set realistic goals
- Improve your understanding of the cognitive processes
- Consider cultural influence
- Create a learning environment for yourself
- Optimize your learning experience
- Support your growth process
- Engage tandem dynamics to get particularly powerful results
- Beware the four dragons of self-leadership
- Improve communication skills
- Improve your cognitive flexibility
- Contribute to your organization
- Remember others as you grow
- Stay open to new outcomes

You can pursue these in any order, although the suggestions are laid out in steps convenient for most people to follow.

Set Realistic Goals

How do we know what to develop? Foremost, our pattern of preferences suggests where to start. If you know your four-letter psychological type code, you can use table 1.2 on pages 8–9 to locate cognitive processes to start developing. The type code is a shortcut label that stands for a pattern of processes.

If you don't know your type code, review your self-assessment results and experiences with the activities in chapters 3 through 10 to help you complete table 11.1. A score of ten or above indicates a likely preference for that process while a score from four to nine indicates a possible supporting preference. Consider that life experience may have guided you to develop or use particular processes. As you review, consider:
- what you have always done well
- what you do frequently and can do very quickly when needed
- what others notice and admire from you
- what you need to still be you

You do not have to settle on a type pattern. It is simply a useful compass to self-leadership. And even if you have decided, each of us develops in a unique way, creating our own paths. Listen to yourself, and you will sense what you care to develop.

TABLE 11.1: Scores for the eight cognitive processes

The 8 Keys to Self-Leadership	Assigned Points
Extraverted Sensing—Immersing in the present context (See page 24)	
Introverted Sensing—Stabilizing with a predictable standard (See page 40)	
Extraverted Intuiting—Exploring the emerging patterns (See page 56)	
Introverted Intuiting—Transforming with a metaperspective (See page 72)	
Extraverted Thinking—Measuring and constructing for progress (See page 88)	
Introverted Thinking—Gaining leverage using a framework (See page 104)	
Extraverted Feeling—Building trust through giving relationships (See page 120)	
Introverted Feeling—Staying true to who you really are (See page 136)	

Also, a few helpful rules of thumb reflect common developmental patterns, though they do not fit for everyone.

TABLE 11.2: Typical development

Age	Typical Development	Example
Child (0–15)	Development of our two preferred processes: lead and support.	Ti and Ne
Youth (15–30)	Synergy between the preferred processes, with a third opposite to the support process. Some awareness of other processes.	Ti, Ne, and Si
Adult (30–50)	Fuller development of processes opposite our preferred process, and a fifth process related to the support process.	Ti, Ne, Si, Fe, and Ni
Elder (50+)	Possible integration of perhaps all eight processes toward a fuller sense of self.	Perhaps all eight processes

Most adults have three processes—though possibly as many as five—that they use with proficiency. Awareness of cognition and ongoing intimate relationships can shift this use. To improve a process, practice the introductory exercises and focus on basic use. Basic use, done well, can add a lot to our lives without creating problems. It is usually better to focus on only a few processes for effective results. Developing a process may take several years.

Improve Your Understanding

The true scope of individual variation is often hard to grasp. How can we really understand a new process when our reference points are the ones we already know? The following exercises have repeatedly been proven to help teach the true scope and value of each process.

Exercise 1

Read one of the chapters on cognitive processes in detail. As you read, record your thoughts. Don't draw conclusions; just record what comes to mind. When you are done, analyze what you wrote to see which processes were evident in your writing. This exercise is particularly useful for finding out how much you use a process.

Exercise 2

Pair with a friend who has different preferences from yours. If you prefer an introverted process as your lead, then try this exercise with someone who has an extraverted preference and vice versa. Each of you write a vignette reflecting a daily activity from a first-person point of view. That is, write about yourself using "I." Choose a work situation if you like. Then put this vignette aside for later. Next, interview your partner about his or her preferences and write a second vignette reflecting a typical day for him or her. Match his or her point of view as closely as possible. Most likely your first attempt will not capture the fullness or style of the other person's experience. Swap the vignettes you initially wrote of yourselves. Use the other person's vignette as a guide to improve your portrayal and try again. A third rewrite may be needed, or choose another situation to write about and repeat the process. You will likely find it easier this time. You might even write a new vignette of yourself incorporating a new process.

Exercise 3

When you have the cognitive processes fairly well in mind, interview people. Take them through chapter 1 and then select two or three processes to explore in more detail. They may wish to explore with you, with someone else, or alone. In any case, ask about and capture their response to the material as you did for yourself in the first exercise. Then analyze their response for signs of their preferences. Feel free to share your own preferences as needed, since comparisons can be very useful. These interviews are similar to what is often called a "360 assessment," when a person gets feedback from many people around him about himself. You may discover that someone you thought you knew well has sides you haven't seen before.

Consider Cultural Influence

We grow up in and are profoundly influenced by our home culture. Research suggests that culture influences how we recognize our cognitive preferences and the opportunities we have to exercise them.

For North American culture, data strongly suggests the mainstream preference is for introverted Sensing. Also, American men are encouraged to develop extraverted Thinking, and American women are encouraged to develop extraverted Feeling. Schooling, particularly university life, also encourages introverted Thinking. This means we may develop basic use of these processes and find ourselves using them a lot, even if we don't prefer them. This is a two-edged sword. On the one hand, if these processes are your preferences, then you have an advantage from the start, but there are few reasons to develop other processes. On the other hand, if you prefer other processes, you have likely developed the culture-influenced processes earlier than you might otherwise have but possibly at the expense of what comes most naturally to you.

Our preferences may run counter to expectations of our gender roles. Women who prefer Thinking processes and men who prefer Feeling processes report lifelong challenges.

Data also suggests these same patterns occur in large organizations, including the military and government. Small organizations tend to emphasize the preferences of their leader or the specific characteristics of the industry. Small, start-up high-technology companies may emphasize Intuiting and Thinking, while care-giving professions may emphasize Sensing and Feeling.

Individuals who prefer extraverted Sensing or extraverted Intuiting have highly open, flowing attention compared to others. In cultures like North America or Northern Europe, the emphasis is often on completing tasks by the clock and focusing for long periods of time. Perceptiveness and responsiveness can be interpreted as a lack of attention and perhaps even cause for medication. In contrast, in more relaxed cultures, a high task focus typical of extraverted Thinking can be interpreted as obsessive or lacking in patience and subtlety.

Other cultures often emphasize different cognitive processes, such as extraverted Sensing or even introverted Intuiting. Discovering cultures that match our preferences can be a life-altering experience.

Create a Learning Environment

Here are some tips to make your explorations more satisfying.

Find a Mentor or Crowd

One of the most powerful ways to learn and grow involves stretching with people who share a process in common with us but also prefer a process that we find hard to use. Spend time with people who prefer the process you are trying to develop or sustain. Ideally this means everyday exposure because a lot of what goes on with each process happens outside our awareness.

Contribute to Something Larger Than Yourself

Often a process is most fully engaged when we use it to create or support an organization, a cause, or a big-picture purpose—that is, advanced use emerges most when we engage in something that energizes us or is larger than ourselves. This is true for processes we are developing as well as for those we naturally prefer.

Nurture New Processes as You Sustain Preferences

Locate a place in your life to incubate and develop a cognitive process. You might explore a hobby or a side venture initially kept separate from work, or you might progressively introduce a process in small ways into your existing work. Starting small allows you to maintain who you are while exploring. A new process is a new resource with new options. Usage adds value, flexibility, and acuity. It also can be awkward or bring surprises. Sometimes people who know the "old you" may resist and express alarm. Be prepared to see the trappings of your old life in a new way!

Cultivate Patience

Accepting that we can grow or flex to use a particular process is one thing; actual growth often takes many years. You might visit one process and return years later to continue developing it. Also, as you improve your use of a process, it may illuminate new paths to follow.

Optimize Your Learning Experience

Even as we develop nonpreferred processes, we grow most when our environment and resources fit our preferred processes. Use the suggestions below to help develop the process or processes you are focusing on. When engaging in a process, people need specific support.

- Extraverted Sensing: We need real-world challenges, such as tackling crisis situations that require our talents and demand that we grow.
- Introverted Sensing: We need sure guidance from mentors who will shepherd and promote us into roles and responsibilities that best suit us.
- Extraverted Intuiting: We need an intelligent atmosphere with bright peers and perceptive mentors who challenge us to develop and test our many ideas.
- Introverted Intuiting: We need creative resources so we can pursue complex projects in an interdisciplinary way, with moderate structure and review and minimal criticism.
- Extraverted Thinking: We need leadership opportunities in which to exercise our ability to manage complex situations that require coordinating people, resources, and systems to meet goals.
- Introverted Thinking: We need a flexible network so we can engage in independent serious thought while conferring with peers and expert mentors for feedback and insights.
- Extraverted Feeling: We need affirmation from the people around us who can identify and encourage our talents in a personal way.
- Introverted Feeling: We need genuine community in which to learn with peers and mentors who share values while encouraging individual self-expression.

Support the Growth Process

Self-leadership is more than developing cognitive processes. Research into the lives of happy, successful people reveals core attitudes and activities that maintain openness to learning and growing. Consider how you can incorporate each of the general activities below into your life to keep growing

As an individual
- Take responsibility for life choices as ongoing commitments.
- Keep learning and increasing your options by exploring new tools and new resources.
- Orient yourself to make creative contributions to your profession.
- Identify and trust your personal creative process, and act on moments of peak energy, creativity, and performance as they come up.
- Engage in the business of living life in multiple areas at once.

As a leader
- Lead across different, opposing groups and in multiple spheres of life instead of leading one group against another.
- Heed the call to make sacrifices for the welfare of all sides of a dispute.
- Help others lead in their own way.
- Allow peace and conflict to coexist by putting into place checks and balances.
- Maintain daily self-testing for humility.

In her writings, Isabel Myers identified other common qualities among high-functioning individuals regardless of their cognitive preferences:[2]
- Confidence in the skill and meaningfulness of our preferences. This requires that we know who we are.
- Willingness to shift, explore, and engage our nonpreferred processes. This means we are open to being who we are not.
- Stamina to continue in the face of failure and obstacles, from rejection of who we are to mistakes we make as we develop.

These qualities are not exclusive to particular processes. Consider ways to develop confidence, flexibility, and stamina in your life.

Engage Processes in Tandem for Powerful Results

Each of the cognitive processes can be used with its opposite in a tandem relationship (see page 20). At first a process and its "opposite" may feel in tension with each other, but with practice you will discover ways to use them together effectively. As you develop a process, you can draw on the examples below to enhance your use and create powerful results.

Extraverted Sensing

We can get powerful results using extraverted Sensing in tandem with introverted Intuiting. We can be very tuned in to the surrounding environment, with anticipation of what's coming next. We may constantly read our industry's current news to be sure to catch the next wave of innovations. Or we can engage people in fun activities, drawing them out and helping them transform themselves. We might pull a shy person onto the dance floor, convinced that she has an inner dancer waiting to be released, so that she can experience her potential firsthand. Or we might shape the current context to what we envision it can be, like a sculptor who can "see" the final statue within a chunk of marble and sculpts everything else away to get to it.

Introverted Sensing

We can get impressive results using introverted Sensing in tandem with extraverted Intuiting. We might have a keen awareness of what has come before and link that knowledge to what might be. This might involve drawing upon a wealth of past experience and sifting through what is known to discover patterns; for example, researching the history of a place in great detail to solve a lingering mystery. We might use allegories from traditional fantasy to pass on important standards and values to the next generation or read mystery novels as a way to relax from the daily grind of work. A little imagination, fantasy, or humor can lighten our daily routine or help make a long-term relationship more enjoyable. Seeing positive possibilities also reassures us when a situation is unstable.

Extraverted Intuiting

We can get impressive results using extraverted Intuiting in tandem with introverted Sensing. We might interpret the meaning of a situation by relating it to images from the past. We see a pattern in the present moment, and in addition to imagining alternative scenarios, we draw upon our memories of the past. This recollection enables us to explore many more situations at once. Similarly, an academic researcher might do extensive research and book study of those who have come before while exploring a theoretical problem. We might embrace the convenience of supportive institutions so that we can live more freely in a world of ideas. We might even dream up a novel way to do something and then establish it as a new tradition or predictable standard for society.

Introverted Intuiting

We can get impressive results using introverted Intuiting in tandem with extraverted Sensing. We might try out various tangible experiences and activities to catalyze realizations for growth. The more varied and undigested experiences one has, the more material there is for the unconscious to draw upon. We might look inward to envision how we can transform something, then gather data and take actions to realize that goal—to make real what is envisioned. For example, we might visualize how people will one day journey into space and then take the actions necessary to design and build a spaceship to accomplish that goal. This might take many years of action, including activities to sustain the vision. Another tandem relationship involves engaging in a physical activity so that body, mind, and environment merge to become one, perhaps experiencing a great sense of calm or energy.

Extraverted Thinking

We can get impressive results using extraverted Thinking in tandem with introverted Feeling. We might sequence and prioritize based on objective measures while following beliefs about what's important. If there isn't enough time in the day to do everything we want, we may select those things that matter most to us. Or perhaps, while trying to make a decision, we discover that the available evidence isn't enough to convince us one way or another. Until we get more evidence, we go with what we believe to be true. Being in touch with what we believe in motivates us to use will power and to follow a procedure or task through to completion. We might structure an organization or system to be as fair as possible, honoring individual identities.

Introverted Thinking

We can get impressive results using introverted Thinking in tandem with extraverted Feeling. We might draw on a nugget of reasoning or theoretical framework to make adjustments for the welfare of others or the good of the group. Applying principles of human behavior and applying leverage at key points can help us to manage divergent values, feelings, and opinions. We might nurture relationships with a network of respected peers while clarifying a framework or disclose personal data to gain clarity and precision for a topic. Or we might feel passionate about the value of people everywhere learning to use a particular framework as a problem-solving tool to improve human relationships. We communicate this framework to others as a helpful gift.

Extraverted Feeling

We can get impressive results using extraverted Feeling in tandem with introverted Thinking. We can connect with others by following guidelines about appropriate behavior. We may follow principles of fair play or the golden rule—a general framework for all our transactions with others. We might locate leverage points in a situation to help all parties get what they need in the most affirming and fair way possible or leverage our range of social contacts to get help or to interact with someone we wouldn't normally have access to. Or we might mediate a dispute between two parties: we observe from multiple angles to fully see every side and give a fair hearing as we fit their claims with a framework to arrive at a decision.

Introverted Feeling

We can get impressive results using introverted Feeling in tandem with extraverted Thinking. We can stay true to our beliefs by structuring our lives and standing firm with what's important. We might decide against purchasing a particular product that harms the environment and then arrange our lives or the organization we lead to make do without it. We might refer to evidence and empirical reasoning to support what we believe is true. Maybe we hold fast to the idea that all people bring useful gifts to society, then construct a sorter or a metric and gather data to demonstrate this value. Or we might use time management and spatial organization skills to better follow through on important commitments and worthwhile projects.

Beware the Four Dragons of Self-Leadership

We all encounter a few major pitfalls when developing the cognitive processes. It's useful to be vigilant regarding these as well as forgiving of ourselves and others. Consider when you tend to get stuck in each of the major pitfalls below and ways to avoid them in the future.

Be Like Me

One pitfall is asking others to do things our way. This is called "Be Like Me."[3] We may labor for years trying to reform colleagues, friends, and loved ones. Or we might insist that our environment, culture, or organization change to suit us. This is usually a hopeless task. People engage their preferences instinctually; to ask others to stop using their lead processes is like asking them to stop breathing. The task is also unnecessary; each process offers a gift well suited to dealing with the world in a particular way. What we can do is encourage people to use their preferred processes in the healthiest and most appropriate ways possible and to be open to adding the use of other processes to better achieve the aims of their lead process.

A variation on this pitfall is to acknowledge that all processes are valuable but insist that only one or two are best suited to a particular organization or a particular project. The question isn't which process is best when but how using each process contributes to understanding and improving the current situation.

Be Like Them

Another pitfall we all encounter is called "Be Like Them." We try to remake ourselves to fit the expectations of those around us. If we already know our preferred processes, this can be very uncomfortable and draining: we can make do but not for long. If we don't know our preferred processes, then we can struggle for energy and direction until we encounter a mirror of ourselves, something that shows us the incongruity in our lives. All families, organizations, and cultures emphasize the use of certain processes; fortunately, a journey of self-discovery appears to be universal and natural.

Master of All

A third pitfall is trying to be good at every process, which is neither possible nor desirable. We become more skilled at using a process by practicing it. To use all processes equally within the limited hours of a day is to become a jack of all trades and a master of none, leading to a life of strife for the people around us. For example, although we might practice giving and receiving to build relationships, if we don't truly invest in our relationships, we may likely misunderstand others' needs and impose our values on them. If we are simultaneously trying to measure and build for progress, we may end up counting something that doesn't need to be counted, making endless lists, and giving reasons for actions without fully investigating the evidence at hand. Nature's path is the right one: develop your natural preferences while giving some attention to your nonpreferred processes.

A variation on this pitfall is to think we're engaging various processes when in fact we're simply doing what we do naturally. For example, it's possible to interpret every cognitive process as a different strategy that looks for certain leverage points. That's fine. But be honest with yourself. Explore the processes. Do the exercises in reality and not just in your imagination. Learning is exciting!

It's Not Me; It's My Preference

This last major pitfall is making excuses for our choices by saying we are servants of our preferences. We might say, "I can't help being impulsive; that's the way I am," or "I can't let go of this bad relationship because that's hard for people like me." This attitude suggests we don't care to grow and want others to change instead to suit our desires.

A variation on this pitfall is asking others to handle everything for us. It's fine to hire or partner with people to cover our weaknesses, but be cautious about relying so much on others that we feel helpless without them. Even as we benefit from staying with our preferences, maturity involves developing our nonpreferred processes.

Improve Communication Skills

Cognitive preferences influence ease of communication and teamwork. People with similar levels of development and use can often get along quite well, while people with significant differences can encounter many challenges. We can represent possible patterns of interaction using the following table.[4]

TABLE 11.3: Illustrating patterns of interaction

Joe's preferences	Possible Links	Jane's preferences
introverted Thinking		extraverted Feeling
extraverted Intuiting		introverted Sensing
introverted Sensing		extraverted Intuiting

Joe prefers introverted Thinking and extraverted Intuiting, with modest development and use of introverted Sensing. In comparison, Jane prefers extraverted Feeling and introverted Sensing, with modest development and use of extraverted Intuiting. He and Jane share two preferences—two ways to communicate—even though their lead processes are quite different. Here are some patterns of interaction:

- We have an instant connection with someone who shares our preferences.

  Both people speak the same language. However, the rapport may not last if maturity or specifics of use differ markedly. For example, Joe and a colleague (Miguel) may both think in terms of ruling frameworks, but what if their frameworks conflict? The result might be a lot of critiquing, defining, and counter-leveraging. Fortunately, both Joe and Miguel will likely remain objective and impersonal about their dialog—unless one of them slips into using another process.

- We have an easy connection with someone who shares one process with us.

For Jane, this means someone who prefers extraverted Feeling or introverted Sensing along with a different process. For example, her close cousin Sandra prefers extraverted Feeling and introverted Intuiting. Matches like this often produce good working relationships that facilitate communication in larger groups. The two people share a preference, and each can act as a bridge to a third party the other seems to have little in common with.

- We have a slow connection with someone whose preferences are opposite to our own.

For Joe, this means a person with preferences for extraverted Feeling and introverted Sensing. Each person may recognize something interesting about the other but often can't quite make a lasting communication connection. When less mature, we may focus on the negative qualities of opposing preferences. When more mature, there is a clear understanding of potential as we wait for bonds to develop. The long-term result can be rewarding.

- We have a difficult connection with people whose preferences compete with our own.

For Jane, this means someone with extraverted Thinking and introverted Intuiting. In these pairings, we may not notice how different the other person's perspective is and can quickly offend each other. Often a third party is needed to bridge differences. Patience and knowledge of the other processes are important.

- We have a variable connection in the remaining combinations.

For Joe, this means working with someone who prefers introverted Intuiting or extraverted Thinking. While Joe and this colleague prefer making decisions according to objective criteria, Joe's criteria are derived from a framework or set of principles, while his colleague's criteria are based on measurement of evidence and empirical reasoning.

Ultimately, relationships depend on individual maturity and capabilities and who has something at stake. Differences may be a constant source of friction if people find themselves unable to shift perspectives.

Or differences may be synergistic, particularly when both people can shift. If only one party is willing to shift, consider this rule of thumb: it becomes the responsibility of the one who will get the most from an interaction to make the necessary shift.

Improve Your Cognitive Flexibility

Each cognitive process is best used when we enter a particular mode, such as the observer mode, the immersive mode, or the empathic mode. A mode is "felt." You'll know when you're in it. But how can we access a mode quickly and easily?

We briefly look at four common modes in the exercise below. This general exercise is useful for understanding how easily you can learn to move from mode to mode. Practicing this exercise will make entering, staying in, and switching modes faster and easier.

Each mode brings us a particular perspective, certain useful information, a look and feel to our actions, and unique challenges. A mode is like the possible points of view in a novel—first-person protagonist, third-person narrator, and so on.

An Introspective Exercise

Take a minute to relax for this exercise. You may prefer to read the entire exercise first and then reread it at a slower pace as you go through it step by step. You can also close your eyes if you find doing that is more comfortable.

Remember something. It could be a memory from this morning or last weekend or seven years ago. Pick a neutral or somewhat positive memory that includes someone else.

From what perspective do you see that memory? From what perspective do you find yourself "re-viewing" the memory? Try to see from all three of the following perspectives:

- Can you see yourself in your memory as if you are a fly on the wall or as if you are watching yourself on film in a movie theater? (This is the third-person perspective, useful for accessing the observer and empirical modes that promote the Thinking processes.)
- Do you reexperience those past events through your own eyes as if you were there again, reliving them? (This is the first-person perspective, useful for accessing immersing and warning modes that promote the Sensing processes.)

• When another person is in the memory, can you empathize, seeing the experience through his or her eyes and physical point of view? (This is the second-person perspective, useful for accessing the listening and empathizing modes that promote the Feeling processes.)

Now try out more memories with more richness and detail. If you can see yourself "on screen," can you hear what was said? When stepping into yourself to see through your own eyes again, what sensations register about how you felt? Were you hungry or sitting uncomfortably? Finally, some people report an easy time stepping into someone else's shoes. From this mode we can easily hear and feel as well as see from the other person's perspective.

A fourth, "meta" point of view is also possible. It allows us to know about, understand, and shift between the other three points of view. (This is the metaperspective, useful for accessing the inference and meditative modes that promote the Intuiting processes.)

Most people experience memories from a default mode related to a preferred cognitive process. And we can change modes when directed. Sometimes a mode may be adopted only with effort or give only partial information. We may even find it hard to believe other people live in a mode different from our own. The magic of these modes is that they are not just about memory and the past. They show us how we experience the present and future as well. They even influence how we experience ourselves.

Your default mode:	
Your hardest mode:	

Contribute to Your Organization

All eight cognitive processes contribute to the essential activities of organizations. With each situation, project, or team, practice looking for how each process can be drawn upon to improve performance and satisfaction. This might mean focusing on the best use of your preferred cognitive processes. Or a situation might require that you use a process you aren't so comfortable with; perhaps no one else can provide it. Or you may need to recruit others to assist you. These situations encourage leadership when you activate yourself and others in a healthy way to work for the best interests of the group.

Extraverted Sensing
- Manage crises with quick responsiveness.
- Make things happen and go around obstacles to get things done.
- Face risks with confidence.
- Handle many projects and activities simultaneously.

Introverted Sensing
- Bring a storehouse of detailed experiences to learn from mistakes.
- Support the organization in detail on a day-to-day basis.
- Have patience for overcoming bureaucratic obstacles, such as government offices or other organizations.
- Absorb and faithfully carry out the organization's training.

Extraverted Intuiting
- Bring new ideas, trends, opportunities, and new clients.
- See the hidden dynamics in an organization.
- Promote and market newly emerging products, services, and ideas.
- Keep the organization networked with other organizations.

Introverted Intuiting
- Conceive a long-term vision with a plan to realize that vision.
- Lay out innovative ways of thinking and organizing.
- See and prevent future problems.
- Guide others to transform in order to fulfill their potential.

Introverted Thinking
- Bring specialized expertise.
- Have energy for and focus on solving challenging problems.
- Locate leverage points by which to maximize results with minimum resource use.
- Be strategic by examining situations from all angles.

Extraverted Thinking
- Organize people and resources for optimal workflow efficiency.
- Set standards by which to evaluate performance.
- Identify and implement the painful choices the organization may face.
- Create procedures, templates, and so on that everyone can follow.

Extraverted Feeling
- Keep members happy by creating a family-like environment.
- Provide attentive and personal customer service.
- Hear and communicate needs, values, and ethics with new and existing members.
- Form alliances and partnerships with other organizations.

Introverted Feeling
- Keep the organization centered on what's important.
- Evoke loyalty and commitment, giving the organization personal meaning.
- Tie the organization to societal concerns and larger issues.
- Communicate what can't be said directly.

Remember Others

Self-leadership involves more than you. As you try new processes, the people around you may express surprise, delight, dismay, and many other diverse reactions. You can recruit their responses as feedback to help you calibrate your choices and changes to keep improving your comfort with a cognitive processes. At the same time, keep in mind that other people's contributions include their biases as well as possible insights, so be sure to solicit feedback from as many people as possible, particularly from those you trust.

When you hear concern from others, let them know that the "old you" isn't gone; you are sampling something new. Also let them know you are trying to be patient with yourself as you learn smoother, more advanced use of a cognitive process. Like a colt learning to walk, genuine transformation can feel awkward and may involve a few bumps and falls. Sometimes, someone may not react positively because of what you are not doing. As you focus on one process you might neglect another. For example, using extraverted Thinking involves making decisions based on objective measurable criteria: if someone doesn't finish a report on time, then it is not on time. This bumps up against the use of extraverted Feeling, which involves how much we like someone and ways to help that person feel good: you might want to overlook that late report. The long-term benefit of self-leadership is that eventually you will learn how to consider both perspectives.

As you go, you may also notice whether other people are benefiting from or perhaps getting hurt by the changes you are making. Then you may want to shift what you are doing. Fortunately, the mind has a life of its own, and you may notice your subconscious guiding you to the best possible use.

Stay Open to New Outcomes

Self-leadership is an ongoing process. Attaining a particular goal can be very satisfying, and on your journey, you will know your efforts are bearing fruit when you discover new kinds of outcomes, refreshing journeys to take, renewed ways to feel satisfied, and new people around you.

Continuing Your Journey

Tips for Using the Eight Keys Together

Learning to use the eight cognitive processes together in a satisfying way is a true test of self-leadership. Until now, we have explored each of the eight processes separately. However, we may use all eight cognitive processes throughout the day and even during a single activity. Learning to use the processes together takes awareness and practice. A good metaphor is Morse-code.[5] To the untrained ear, the code is a confusion of noise. To the trained ear, the dots and dashes relate words, and thus sentences and meanings. Learning to translate the code as we are hearing it takes acuity and practice. So too does learning to translate the eight keys into everyday tasks as we are doing them. There are three important steps to master using the eight keys together. With each activity, we need to

1. Perceive which cognitive processes we and others are using
2. Consider our level of comfort and skill with each process
3. Decide what kind of cooperative relationships are possible

We will explore twelve tips for better usage, from learning to focus on the process rather than behavior and differentiating low-key from high-key use of a process to noticing catalytic relationships between people's use of processes.

Focus on the Core Process, Not Behaviors

We do things for many reasons. Two people may behave the same way, but they use different cognitive processes toward their own ends. The behavior serves an underlying motivation. The following example illustrates this.

TABLE 12.1: Behavior: tidying a desk

Process	Approach
extraverted Thinking	A desire for order in the outer world that is efficient for productivity and makes it easier to control one's environment (measuring and using a template).
extraverted Feeling	A desire to please other people, such as office mates, or to fulfill social values about how to maintain a proper desk (giving in a relationship).
extraverted Sensing	A desire to convey a particular image, impact, style, or impression to create a physically comfortable or aesthetically pleasing workspace (shaping an aesthetic environment).

Many activities serve the core of a process, giving a great variety of expression. So ask and explore why something is done a certain way instead of relying on outward behaviors. You might even offer specific choices, such as "Does this desk match who you are as a person?" or "Are you following a specific framework, such as optimal workflow efficiency?"

Clarify What's Happening

Often two cognitive processes address a similar situational need in opposite ways. This means the two processes probably cannot be engaged together well. The following example illustrates this situation.

TABLE 12.2: Need: to perceive what's happening right now

Process	Approach
extraverted Sensing	Perceive tangible data, notice potential options to take action, and seek immersion in the immediate context. Flow in the here and now and navigate the tangible environment.
extraverted Intuiting	Perceive conceptual data and inferences, notice potential to consider, and seek immersion in a flow that links data from outside the context. Go with ideas as they come up in the moment.

Because of the surface similarities of the two processes, we may need to ask questions to find out what's happening. Many basic ways we use a process are not obvious. Jane is looking, but what is she seeing? The employees are listening, but what are they listening for and what do they hear? You may need to explicitly ask, such as requesting feedback through a summary report of observations or learnings.

As another example, consider extraverted Thinking and extraverted Feeling. Rob and Jane have been sent to fill the same managerial or instructional role, but they work in opposite ways. Rob is attending to everyone's needs and values, concerned about people's feelings. He is giving and receiving to build relationships. Meanwhile, Jane is attending to whether people are working productively and what they need to get back on track. She is monitoring and arranging their roles according to an organizational template.

Think in Terms of Change

The cognitive processes are dynamic and use shifts from moment to moment. Often we do not stay engaged in one process for a long time. We rapidly move from using one to using another. So look for differences, change, and variation, as the following example illustrates.

TABLE 12.3: Activity: Finding one's way to an unfamiliar location

Process	Approach
extraverted Sensing	Walking around and looking to see where you are now; noticing physical clues, such as signs or paths.
extraverted Thinking	Comparing the features on a map to the physical scene around you; paying attention to how much time you have.
introverted Intuiting	Experiencing a sudden aha about which direction you must go, even with an incomplete map and limited observables.

You might prefer processes different from these three to navigate. The point is that while engaged in an activity, we often move back and forth between processes in order to meet a need or goal. The more processes available to us, the better equipped we are for success.

To better understand processes, it is helpful to compare and contrast them with each other and to use verbs to think about processes instead of using nouns or adjectives. For example, use "moving around" instead of "active" or use "focusing on details" instead of "meticulous." Also, it is easier to notice processes after they have been used, so reflect on how you have done things in the past. You can take a guess about which process was operating and then check out the evidence. With practice you will learn to observe and test the processes while you are using them.

Distinguish Preference from Skill

People can develop skills. A career or long-term role might strongly encourage us to use a particular process, even if it is not our favorite. We might even explore a process for a while in lieu of using an innate preference as we seek greater understanding and overall satisfaction in life. In short, preferences influence behavior and we develop beyond our preferences, as the following example illustrates.

TABLE 12.4: Process: introverted intuiting

Level of use	How we use and experience the process
Innate preference	Since childhood, have often experienced sudden realizations or insights; as an adult, may engage in reframing and mind shifting every few minutes.
Learned skill	As a teen or adult, learned and practiced various forms of meditation, or maybe learned visioning and reframing as leadership techniques in school.

Consider a musician. Preference is similar to talent, and skill comes from practice. When neither is present, then the cognitive process is missing from the person's repertoire and there are likely blind spots and a sense of a smaller set of choices. Practice alone is great, but we often feel that something is missing from the performance. The process is "learned" and perhaps "forced." In contrast, talent alone is a wonderful gift that feels natural but begs for further development. When it's not developed (for whatever reason), then we feel a sense of lost potential.

The cognitive process is engaged at its full potential and is as appealing as a fine musican when both talent and skill are evident.

Distinguish Basic from Advanced Use

Sometimes it seems like we engage a process in an advanced way, but close observation reveals a lack of basic use. At other times we see someone engage a process in an advanced way and wonder how we could possibly do that. Fortunately, everyone has basic use of all eight processes, and basic use improves advanced use for more satisfying results, as the example on the following page illustrates.

TABLE 12.5: Process: extraverted feeling

Level of use	How we use and experience the process
Basic (passive and cultural)	Feel pulled to be responsible and take care of others' feelings and make people feel comfortable by engaging in hosting and caretaking.
Advanced (active and unique)	Easily take on someone else's needs and values as our own. Easily communicate personally with all persons in a group to feel at one with them.

With extraverted Feeling, when we enter an empathic mode, we are paying attention to others' needs, values, feelings, and relationships with others. Sometimes we can just feel this pull, and at other times we engage in activities such as hosting as a way to get to know people better (as well as giving them something). If we don't know someone well, then we certainly can't take on their needs!

Keep in mind that basic use is a prerequisite for advanced use, just as being a sapling is a prerequisite for becoming an adult tree. Advanced use without basic use often leads to disruptive or disappointing results. And even before basic use, we must enter into the appropriate mode for best use of that process. For example, satisfying use of introverted Feeling requires we enter a mode of listening to others and to our conscience. If we miss this step and forget to listen, then we may likely apply our convictions in a rigid way to a situation.

Sort Look-Alike Experiences

The cognitive processes may look alike to ourselves or others. Some processes can look alike in several ways, as the following example illustrates.

TABLE 12.6: Experience: you feel a strong kinesthetic sense

Process	Approach
introverted Sensing	An information source informs our decisions. A series of past impressions comes to mind unbidden, and maybe we make a comparison that leaves us feeling something now differs from the past.
introverted Feeling	This judging process uses different sources of information as checkpoints to evaluate what's important while making choices. We often feel something is right or wrong without verbalizing.

What is misleading here is the visceral experience we have of both processes. All cognitive processes can be experienced in a visual, auditory, or kinesthetic (feeling) way.

As another example, uses of introverted Thinking and introverted Feeling can look very similar to an outside observer. Both are decision-making processes. We use them quietly in our inner mental world, which makes it hard for others to distinguish between them. Using either process, we might talk about "principles." Also, both processes may appear flexible until something violates a core precept. Then both can be expressed intensely with a fair amount of emphasis. But there is a dramatic difference between them. Introverted Thinking is impersonal. We use the process to figure out the operating principles of the world around us. Ideally, a law of physics or principle of effective sales is not biased by personal beliefs and captures the essence of how something works. Gravity isn't "important." It just is. In contrast, introverted Feeling is personal. We choose to live with our individual convictions and commitments. Even when a belief is about something universal, such as the need for compassion for all living things, our personal commitment to this universal principle comes first.

TABLE 12.7: Behavior: a person strongly expresses something important

Process	Approach
introverted Thinking	We reference and refine a ruling mental framework in a detached objective way, devoid as much as possible of anything personal that might bias analysis and understanding. The framework might describe values in a universal way.
introverted Feeling	What and how we choose to believe is very personal and subjective. Our choices become the fabric of our personal identity. Beliefs might be about something universal, such as the need for peace.

Each cognitive process has many activities that follow logically from a core principle that we don't see or experience directly. Even when introspecting, consider that two processes might look alike.

Differentiate Low-Key from High-Key Use

Given a choice, people use their preferred processes. However, the situation, our culture or current mood, or social pressure (such as the presence of a manager or parent) can influence how we express our preferred processes. For example, if we are attending a music concert we may focus on using extraverted Sensing in a passive way, taking in the richness of the music, rather than using extraverted Sensing in a more active way (say, getting up and dancing). Or if we are sitting in an office meeting and are new to the company, we may start brainstorming ideas using extraverted Intuiting but decide to keep these ideas to ourselves until a particularly good one comes along to share. From the perspective of others at the meeting, we only spoke once; in fact, we were using extraverted Intuiting in an active—but quiet—way. The lesson is that each process can be used in a low-key or high-key way. Low-key is quiet and contained, using nonverbal behavior to communicate, such as raising an eyebrow, or perhaps speaking or acting only once at the most opportune moment. When we use a process in a low-key way, our perceptions and decisions are kept private. In contrast, high-key is loud and energetic, often using words and unmistakable actions to communicate. Decision making and information gathering are done out loud in an obvious, public way. So as you observe others or consider how to engage a process, consider whether high-key or low-key is the most fitting for the situation.

Consider Interpersonal Dynamics

Cognitive processes are not just in the head. We engage them with other people. Usage is contextual and varies with the processes others use, as table 12.8 and table 12.9 illustrate.

Jane and Mary Give a Presentation Together

Mary and Jane both often use extraverted Intuiting and will likely do so in their presentation. They are both comfortable following a flow of questions and ideas from the audience and taking a couple of detours along the way that seem fun.

However, Jane's use is mainly basic, while Mary's includes both basic and advanced use. Whenever the situation exceeds Jane's ability with extraverted Intuiting, she will likely switch to a process she prefers more, such as introverted Sensing; at the same time, Mary will be tempted to pick up where Jane left off and continue with more advanced extraverted Intuiting. If someone suggests an alternative interpretation of what Jane and Mary are presenting, Mary is more likely to engage in brainstorming, while Jane is more likely to return to the established interpretation. The situation can go from the facilitators' being in synch to their being opposed to each other in a single moment.

Jane and Mary's other preferred processes may usefully cover each other's weaknesses or generate conflict. Jane may focus too much on a familiar way to do a presentation, while Mary might think a basic outline and attention to the clock are all that's needed.

Also, neither of them prefers three other processes, which are potential blind spots:
- How is the physical environment they are presenting in impacting them and their audience? (extraverted Sensing)
- What is their vision for how the presentation will transform the people in the audience? (introverted Intuiting)
- Is the content of their presentation consistent and logical, or is it a bunch of material thrown together that sounds good? (introverted Thinking)

TABLE 12.8: Shared situation: Jane's preferences (top three)

Process	Preferred Activity
extraverted Feeling	Share certain values and consider what makes the audience most comfortable.
introverted Sensing	Recall past lessons about presentations and reliable ways to present.
extraverted Intuiting	Have a little fun and be open to jokes and ideas so people don't get bored.

TABLE 12.9: Shared situation: Mary's preferences (top three)

Process	Preferred Activity
extraverted Intuiting	Go with the flow of ideas and facilitate the potential that emerges from dialog.
introverted Feeling	Stay with an inner sense of what is most important to say, regardless if people like it or not.
extraverted Thinking	Do a little organizing up-front so the presentation stays within the allotted time.

Now imagine a third person enters the dynamic—say, a talkative audience member who prefers introverted Thinking. Perhaps this person voices a troublesome issue or asks for a definition for a term being used. If Mary's or Jane's basic use of this process is enough to allow her to respond, then the interaction can continue; otherwise, this is a good example of when to defer an interaction to another time.

Notice Cooperative Relationships

An incredible range of activities can be described and accessed by looking at cooperation between processes. Table 12.10 shows just a few examples of engaging a lead process with a support process.

TABLE 12.10: Lead process: extraverted sensing

Support Process	Cooperative Result
introverted Feeling	Notice opportunities for action and decide if something is significant and worth the effort.
introverted Thinking	Experience the physical world to figure out the basic principles on which something works.
introverted Intuiting	Accumulate experiences and conceptualize new ways of seeing and experiencing things.

Cooperation yields many qualities. For example, when we look at extraverted Sensing with introverted Feeling as preferred processes, we see a richer pattern. A person flows with a sense of pace, rhythm, and process, with quick and easy responses to situations, and often has personal style. He or she is a hands-on, experiential learner and is good at asking questions, offering suggestions, presenting ideas, creating products, and making helpful comments. This person notices and gets in synch with nonverbal information and shows spontaneous and genuine expression. Each of these qualities reflects an awareness of personal identity and what's important to one's self and for others, in an immediately relevant, tangible, and helpful way.

Notice Convergent Relationships

Introverted and extraverted aspects of a process, used together, can support and confirm each other. For example, someone who prefers extraverted Intuiting may feel stuck and lack interesting input for exciting new ideas. A solution is to pair with someone who prefers introverted Intuiting, who can tap into "the unconscious" to generate novel thoughts to play with and vice versa. The two sides of a process can compensate for shortcomings, help narrow or expand options, and create highly effective results. Table 12.11 illustrates this relationship.

Sometimes one person can use both processes to good effect, but most often convergence results from two people working together. One person might have introverted Intuiting in a lead role and the other

TABLE 12.11: Activity: catching future trends

Process	Result of Use
introverted Intuiting	We experience an impression about the future or suddenly realize how a future technology or other change will be received. However, the event is often too far into the future or our insight is too different to be useful now.
extraverted Intuiting	We notice hidden dynamics, such as how soon an existing trend will expire, or we bring together things from different contexts in a novel way. However, our idea may be perceived as before its time or too vague for people to be comfortable with.
convergent Intuiting	We notice a trend just before it's about to happen and perhaps intervene to take great advantage of that trend.

person might have extraverted Intuiting in a lead role. They must also share knowledge of the subject at hand! This catalytic dynamic is not the same as teamwork. Healthy teams often have members with varied preferred processes. Rather, this dynamic tends to occur only when the two processes are being used exclusively without interference from any other processes.

Notice Catalytic Relationships

Introverted and extraverted aspects of a process, used together, can generate a back-and-forth catalytic behavior. Each process builds on the other toward something really rich.

Imagine a man picks up a bent twig and a straight twig while hiking and indicates that they have symbolic significance. This is a use of introverted Intuiting.

His hiking partner then uses extraverted Intuiting to generate a number of humorous and insightful possible meanings, such as the straight twig indicating conventional art compared to the bent twig indicating modern art, perhaps wondering which twig they could get more money for if they set up shop and called them art. Or the twigs symbolize two hikers.

A little bit later, the hiker who is using introverted Intuiting reframes these conceptual relationships. He moves to a metaperspective for greater meaning. He realizes that generating metaphors using ordinary objects could be a good way to teach people how to do extraverted Intuiting.

Notice Competing Relationships

What happens when we don't use a process at all? The rejected process may play a negative role as the dominating process tries to handle everything. This is like trying to hammer a nail using only one hand.

For example, both extraverted Sensing and extraverted Intuiting are used in the here and now and are perceiving in nature. But when extraverted Intuiting dominates the situation and extraverted Sensing is not in use, we may

- Talk or ruminate about potential actions but put off action or act in a chaotic, disjointed way.
- Have intuitions about the physical environment instead of engaging it directly. (For example, in the morning we imagine we smell breakfast but don't actually smell anything.)
- Shut out unpleasant sensations and the body's demands instead of uniting with the body. (For example, we exercise a lot but in our mind we disassociate while we exercise.)
- Engage in behavior that doesn't fit the present context. (For example, we eat food while trying to swim or wear shorts when we're cold in the dead of winter.)
- Bring in outside contexts but not the current one; what's out of sight is most on our minds. (For example, we talk business at concerts and concert music at work.)

Compensating is an inevitable result of preference. Trying to engage a nonpreferred process in an advanced way can in fact be perilous since we likely don't have skill there. Fortunately, we always have basic access to a process as part of being human. Taking a moment to engage a nonpreferred process in a basic way can give us very important information. This information may improve the results of our preferred process.

History of and Evidence for Cognitive Processes

Insights into the Theory and Results of Statistical Research

What is the cognitive processes model based on? And are the processes real? Why are there eight and not nine, twelve, or an infinite number? The following discussion isn't meant to completely cover the full scope and depth of the model. Rather, I hope to give you a taste of the fascinating history behind the processes and the research that led to this book.

In the Beginning

In the 1920s, Swiss psychiatrist Carl Jung first described what he called eight psychological functions in his well-known book *Psychological Types*.[6]

Introversion and Extraversion

Jung explored how individuals relate to their social and physical environment and the "objects" in it. Objects might be tools, people, laws, situations, and so on. He noticed that people tend to be either introverted or extraverted in how they relate to these objects. He defined specific meanings:

- Extraversion means that the individual focuses his or her interest on objects in the environment, often adding something "extra." For example, an extravert might use materials to build buildings, meet people and encourage a network of social contacts, or view evidence and try to convince others in a conversation using logical reasoning. The extravert is grounded in the world and is comfortable engaging it.
- Introversion means the individual withdraws from direct interaction with objects and focuses on his or her subjective experience.

The introvert is grounded in his or her internal experience or explanation of the objects and is comfortable engaging this inner world. For example, an introvert might respond to a color's beauty based on what it reminds him or her of, what it symbolizes, what principles it demonstrates, or how it fits with a particular belief.

Jung saw these two qualities as describing the whole person, not just as behaviors. An introvert engages the environment, for example, but she engages it in a way that fits with her inner world and focus on subjective experience.

Four Basic Psychological Functions

What is a "function?" Jung got this term from mathematics, where a function is an equation. For example, a physics equation can describe how a ball moves through the air; we can use the same equation to describe any object's movement. Essentially, a function describes a process that holds true for many specific situations. Similarly, a psychological function describes how we perceive or make decisions (how we orient ourselves to live life). Jung observed four basic functions: Sensing, Intuiting, Thinking, and Feeling. Jung's definitions are complex and nuanced, and only the barest bones are repeated here:

- Sensing (S)—we focus on tangible, experiential awareness of what is, including our internal bodily reactions to what we experience. ("What is" includes the past and what is known factually to us.)
- Intuiting (N)—we focus on symbolic, conceptual awareness of patterns, interrelationships, and potential, influenced and brought to us by the unconscious. (This often results in a sense of what might be or what will be.)
- Thinking (T)—we conceptually connect things (thoughts, objects, feelings, actions, ideas, etc.) to each other, resulting in decisions based on objective criteria, logical theory, and impersonal principles.
- Feeling (F)—we relate something to ourselves, accepting or rejecting what fits our sense of self (ego), resulting in decisions based on appropriateness, values and importance or worth to self and others.

Jung called Sensing and Intuiting "irrational" because they are driven by perception, focused on gathering information and responding fluidly to what is perceived. In contrast, he called Thinking and Feeling "rational" because they are self-consistent ways of judging, organizing, and deciding.

A Total of Eight Psychological Functions

Jung noticed that people grow psychologically—a process he called "individuation." And as people mature, they come to prefer one function (Sensing, Intuiting, Thinking, or Feeling). This function becomes dominant in either an introverted or an extraverted attitude. Thus, he identified eight categories or "types" of people.

Why do we have a type? Jung believed our type results from how we balance three major factors: human instincts, societal demands, and our individual strengths. Our type is how we handle universal human instincts (hunger, sex, curiosity, love, ambition, etc.) against specific social and cultural demands (going to school, joining the army, getting married, etc.) in a way that best suits our natural strengths (having athletic, mathematical, or musical talent, for example.)

Students of Jung have read deeper, resulting in more specific interpretations of how we mature in our use of the functions. Specifically, it appears Jung proposed that a differentiated function is active, whereas an undifferentiated function is passive. For example, differentiated extraverted Thinking involves structuring and managing one's environment according to logical criteria, measurable evidence, and so on. In contrast, undifferentiated use might mean following a structure without adjusting it to the current situation or maybe picking a more effective structure to follow. This results in orderly but foolish behavior.

Auxiliary Functions

Jung proposed that for each of the eight functional types, an auxiliary function usually supports the dominant. The auxiliary function would not compete with the dominant and would be different in every way.[7] Someone with dominant introverted Sensing might have auxiliary extraverted Thinking or auxiliary extraverted Feeling. Jung encouraged his students to help people develop use of their auxiliary functions to give them strength when dealing with personal (shadow) issues.

The Dynamic Tension of Opposites

Jung described how the functions exist in dynamic tension (Sensing versus Intuiting, Thinking versus Feeling) and as we mature, especially at midlife, we may integrate opposite functions. Someone who prefers introverted Intuiting may initially be closed to using extraverted Sensing, finding it unpleasant, difficult, and unrewarding. This would result in one-sided behavior in many situations. But opposites can become partners. The introverted Intuitive can find wholeness by accepting extraverted Sensing in his or her life. Jung saw this process as difficult and fraught with peril, but those after him have considered this a rewarding path for individuals who are psychologically ready. This is a journey to find one's own unique balance in life instead of just meeting the demands of the world around us. Jung believed that psychological dysfunction would result without the compensating balance of one's opposite function and that this compensation happened naturally and could not be forced.[8] He also proposed that some functions compete too much to be helpful. For example, extraverted Intuiting and extraverted Sensing cannot satisfactorily coexist.[9, 10]

A Four-Letter Code for Sixteen Types

In the late 1940s Isabel Myers created the first version of the well-known Myers-Briggs Type Indicator® (MBTI®) instrument. She wanted to bring Jung's ideas to a mass audience. If people knew their dominant function, they could make more informed career and relationship choices. Myers followed the idea that people have two preferred functions—a dominant and an auxiliary. The result was a self-reflective, paper-and-pencil questionnaire that would report a four-letter code. The first three letters were relatively easy:

- Extravert, E   or   Introvert, I
- Sensing, S   or   Intuiting, N (using N since I was taken)
- Thinking, T   or   Feeling, F

But how to determine which function is dominant and which is auxiliary? Myers tapped into a fourth dichotomy she saw in Jung's work:

- Judging, J   or   Perceiving, P

A code such as "INFP" points to one of sixteen whole patterns. The instrument result is a data point to help people find out which type fits them best.

Since Isabel Myers began the process, the instrument has been rigorously tested, and later versions have benefited from much research even as Jung's original theory has been largely lost on many people. Also, theorists have aligned other models to the sixteen types framework. Table A.1 Themes of the sixteen personality types summarize the sixteen types in a holistic way.

A Modern Renaissance

Since Isabel Myers, other people have examined Jung's theory in light of clinical practice, research results, and even insights into brain function. Some have come to differing conclusions, but much research—such as introversion and extraversion observed as amount of sensory stimulation versus brain activity—has validated the worth of Jung's original ideas. Besides neurological studies, cognitive social science has contributed to our understanding. This is one reason why Jung's psychological functions are now referred to as cognitive processes. Many of these modern principles are included in this book, such as the principles of

- Situated Action—Cognition doesn't take place just in the head. We "think" by actively using our environment. For example, we make lists and refer to books to remember ideas. Or if we need to navigate a large building, we aren't dependent on a pre-drawn map. We can look for signs, ask directions, and consider likely options.
- Social Exchange—People generally don't live in isolation. We interact by exchanging goods and services, and we build alliances and trust by doing so. For example, when we buy food at the grocery store, we trust that the money we give the cashier will go to the store and not into the cashier's pocket, just as the cashier trusts that we are not sneaking out anything.
- Metacognition—People don't just think. We think about thinking itself! Our sense of consciousness allows us to evaluate our thoughts, feelings, actions, and so on. For example, we can listen to our conscience to evaluate if our reasoning is just a convenient rationalization to get what we want, or if we are putting forth a genuine argument for something more important.

TABLE A.1: Themes of the sixteen personality types

Foreseer Developer (INFJ)	Harmonizer Clarifier (INFP)
Personal growth. Sustain the vision. Honoring the gifts of others. Taking a creative approach to life. Talent for foreseeing. Exploring issues. Bridge differences and connect people. Practical problem solving. Live with a sense of purpose. Living an idealistic life often presents them with a great deal of stress and a need to withdraw.	Going with the flow. Knowing what is behind what is said. Uncovering mysteries. Exploring moral questions. Talent for facilitative listening. Relate through stories and metaphors. Balancing opposites. Getting reacquainted with themselves. Have a way of knowing what is believable. Struggling with structure and getting their lives in order.
Envisioner Mentor (ENFJ)	**Discoverer Advocate (ENFP)**
Communicate and share values. Succeeding at relationships. Realizing dreams—their own and others. Seek opportunities to grow together. Heeding the call to a life work or mission. Enjoy the creative process. Intuitive intellect. Reconcile the past and the future. Talent for seeing potential in others. Often find living in the present difficult.	Inspiring and facilitating others. Exploring perceptions. Talent for seeing what's not being said and voicing unspoken meanings. Seek to have ideal relationships. Recognize happiness. Living out stories. Want to authentically live with themselves. Respond to insights in the creative process. Finding the magical situation. Restless hunger for discovering their direction.
Conceptualizer Director (INTJ)	**Designer Theorizer (INTP)**
Maximizing achievements. Drive for self-mastery. Build a vision. Very long-range strategizing. Realizing progress toward goals. Systems thinking. Talent for seeing the reasons behind things. Being on the leading edge. Maintaining independence. Find it difficult to let go in interacting with others.	Becoming an expert. Seeing new patterns and elegant connections. Talent for design and redesign. Crossing the artificial boundaries of thought. Activate the imagination. Clarifying and defining. Making discoveries. Reflect on the process of thinking itself. Detach to analyze. Struggle with attending to the physical world.
Strategist Mobilizer (ENTJ)	**Explorer Inventor (ENTP)**
Being a leader. Maximize talents. Marshal resources toward progress. Intuitive explorations. Forging partnerships. Mentoring and empowering. Talent for coordinating multiple projects. Balance peace and conflict. Predictive creativity. Often overwhelmed by managing all the details of time and resources.	Being inventive. Talented at building prototypes and getting projects launched. Lifelong learning. Enjoy the creative process. Share their insights about life's possibilities. Strategically formulate success. An inviting host. Like the drama of the give and take. Trying to be diplomatic. Surprised when their strategizing of relationships becomes problematic.

Planner Inspector (ISTJ)	Protector Supporter (ISFJ)
Drawing up plans and being prepared. Take responsibility. Getting work done first. Being active in the community. Loyalty to their roles. Cultivating good qualities. Doing the right thing. Bear life's burdens and overcome adversity. Talented at planning, sequencing, and noticing what's missing. Having to learn so much in hindsight is painful at times.	Noticing what's needed and what's valuable. Talent for careful and supportive organization. Know the ins and outs. Enjoy traditions. Work to protect the future. Listening and remembering. Being nice and agreeable. Unselfish willingness to volunteer. Feeling a sense of accomplishment. Exasperated when people ignore rules and don't get along.
Implementor Supervisor (ESTJ)	**Facilitator Caretaker (ESFJ)**
Talent for bringing order to chaotic situations. Educating themselves. Industrious, work-hard attitude. Balance work with play. Having a philosophy of life. Having the steps to success. Keeping up traditions. Being well balanced. Connecting their wealth of life experiences. Often disappointed when perfectionistic standards for economy and quality are not met.	Accepting and helping others. Managing people. Hearing people out. Voicing concerns and accommodating needs. Admire the success of others. Remember what's important. Talented at providing others with what they need. Keep things pleasant. Maintaining a sense of continuity. Accounting for the costs. Often disappointed by entrepreneurial projects.
Analyzer Operator (ISTP)	**Composer Producer (ISFP)**
Actively solving problems. Observing how things work. Talent for using tools for the best approach. Need to be independent. Act on their hunches or intuitions. Understanding a situation. Taking things apart. Making discoveries. Sharing those discoveries. Unsettled by powerful emotional experiences.	Taking advantage of opportunities. Stick with what's important. Talent for pulling together what is just right. Creative problem solving. Building relationships. Attracting the loyalties of others. Being their own true self. Have their own personal style. Play against expectations. Struggle with nurturing their own self-esteem.
Promoter Executer (ESTP)	**Motivator Presenter (ESFP)**
Taking charge of situations. Tactical prioritizing. Talent for negotiating. Want a measure of their success. Keep their options open. Enjoy acting as a consultant. Winning people over. Caring for family and friends. Enjoy exhilaration at the edge. Disappointed when others don't show respect.	Stimulating action. Have a sense of style. Talent for presenting things in a useful way. Natural actors—engaging others. Opening up people to possibilities. Respect for freedom. Taking risks. A love of learning, especially about people. Genuine caring. Sometimes misperceive others' intentions.

These principles and others inspired the descriptions in this book of the eight cognitive processes. Every attempt was made to include the full inventory of principles and observations from cognitive social science and to define the "keys" in a way that still honored Jung's original observations and the definitions proposed by other theorists after him.

Eight Essential Frameworks

You probably noticed a diagram near the start of each chapter on the cognitive processes. The diagrams illustrate a cognitive science approach to Jung's ideas. Cognitive science focuses on how our minds are organized, how we represent the world, and how we function mentally. Keeping with this focus, each of the eight cognitive processes is defined as a unique "representation system."

What is a representation system? Consider an example. English speakers use a system called the alphabet to represent sounds. When we string letters together we make words and sentences that impart meaning. The symbols C and A and T by themselves mean nothing, but together they refer to a very popular pet. In contrast, Chinese speakers use a different representation system based on thousands of unique characters. Each character has a sound (many characters may have the same sound), and each character also has a special meaning. There is a unique character just for "cat." If we compare the two systems, English is quick to learn because it has only twenty-six letters, but Chinese has an extra layer of nuance and visual beauty. Each system tackles the same challenge (reading and writing) in a different way and has benefits along with drawbacks.

In the same way, we have different ways to mentally represent the world around us and our place in it, and each system has its strengths and weaknesses. For example, at the core of extraverted Thinking is the concept of measurement. Many aspects of life can be usefully measured and sorted. In contrast, at the core of extraverted Feeling is the concept of social exchange. Many aspects of life can be represented in terms of couples and social networks, such as arrangements like marriage, which cannot truly be understood by numbers alone! Yet when we use extraverted Feeling, we tend to maintain a count of what we've done for others and what they've done for us. The lesson is that we can use any cognitive process to handle life's challenges, whether counting or cohabitating, but some processes are more suited than others for particular tasks.

If the core of each process is a unique representation system, then we can't say "extraverted Sensing is about gathering facts" or "introverted Feeling is about holding beliefs" because facts and beliefs are just content, and content can be used in many ways. When using introverted Feeling, we organize beliefs, facts, perceptions, values, tastes, feelings, and other data according to a very broad flexible representation system called our "personal identity." We then describe, refine, refer to, align, and share our personal identity and its content.

TABLE A.2: Cognitive snapshot of introverted feeling

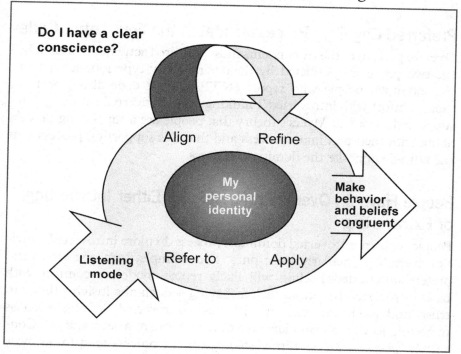

We can fully understand a cognitive process when we understand the representation system at its core. Actions, affect, and attitudes flow naturally from the processes we use because we tend to do what fits with them. Select tools, institutions, and habits afford and enhance use. Learning modes and physiological states help us enter and sustain a process. And we find ways to calibrate (self-correct) that also fit well. Each chapter of this book describes what flows from and supports the core of each process.

Results of a Research Study

After reviewing brain research and gaining firsthand experience observing people in the classroom and in workshops, I created a 120-item questionnaire to study people's use and development of cognitive processes. I analyzed people's responses. The results revealed many clear statistical patterns that match observation as well as revealing a few new patterns. For more information you can visit http://www.cognitiveprocesses.com.

Preferred Cognitive Processes Match the Four-Letter Code

Over 90 percent of the respondents most preferred activities that matched the two processes predicted by their personality type four-letter code. For example, people who report INTP as their code also report the most comfort with introverted Thinking and extraverted Intuiting. This supports Jung's and Myers's theory that people use a supporting process along with their dominant process and that this supporting process is in the attitude opposite the dominant process.

People Have an Overall Preference for Either Introverting or Extraverting

People with an introverted dominant process do more introverted activities overall, particularly basic ones. For example, someone who most prefers introverted Feeling will likely report moderate comfort with basic introverted Intuiting, such as having sudden aha insights they can trust, and moderate comfort with basic introverted Sensing, such as reviewing lots of information over time to confirm a set standard. Conversely, people with an extraverted dominant process tend to do more basic extraverted activities overall.

Some Aspects of a Process Link to a Supporting Process

In addition to basic and advanced aspects of the dominant process, specialized use emerges specific to the supporting process. Everyone who most prefers introverted Thinking will relate to most of the same aspects of this process. However, those who also prefer extraverted Sensing report taking things apart to figure out the principles on which they work, while those who also prefer extraverted Intuiting report juggling and referencing multiple frameworks at once while problem solving.

Processes Have Basic and Advanced Aspects

Almost everyone (over 98 percent) reported more comfort with basic activities than advanced ones overall. That is, people have an easier time with passive activities, such as taking in sensory data or quoting a definition they've learned, than with active activities, such as shaping their physical environment or using a leverage point to solve a problem. Terms like notice and follow were used to construct questionnaire items that assessed basic, passive use. Terms like create and evaluate were used to construct items that assessed active use.

There Are Four Functions, but People Strongly Prefer One Attitude of Their Lead Function

Jung originally proposed four functions: Sensing, Intuiting, Thinking, and Feeling. Other studies suggest people who prefer a function in one attitude (introverted or extraverted) also prefer the other: someone with introverted Feeling as a dominant process would likely engage extraverted Feeling too. The first iteration of the questionnaire showed this result. However, when phrases such as "look inward to" and "in the environment" were added to items in a later version of the questionnaire, this pattern lessened and preference for the preferred function in the opposite attitude often became low. These added phrases appear to clarify the meaning of the questionnaire items as referring to internal or external use. Previous studies may have used unclear items.

Processes Paralleling the Preferred Process Are the Least Preferred

The processes opposite in nature to the preferred ones but occupying the same attitude are significantly least preferred by almost everyone (over 95 percent). For example, someone who prefers introverted Sensing and extraverted Feeling (say, an ESFJ) will most likely have least comfort with introverted Intuiting and extraverted Thinking (typical of, say, INTJ). This helps resolve a question: the tertiary function develops in the same attitude as the dominant process. Previous studies may have used items that did not clarify whether processes were being used internally or externally.

A Process and Its Opposite Can Be Used in Tandem

People can relate to tandem activities. For example, people who prefer extraverted Intuiting report using introverted Sensing in a tandem role, as when they interpret the meaning of a situation fed by related images from the past. The process "opposite" to our lead function is not so opposite!

Process Preference Links to Self-Reflection

People with a preference for extraverted Intuiting report the widest use of various cognitive processes, perhaps overestimating their use. People with a preference for introverted Sensing report the narrowest use of various cognitive processes, perhaps underestimating their use.

Woman Rate Feeling Higher, Men Rate Thinking Higher

Jung hypothesized some tendencies related to gender, and decades of research using the Myers-Briggs Type Indicator® questionnaire supports the observation that more men than women prefer Thinking, while more women than men prefer Feeling. We found that men and women come in all types but gender tendencies exist. Both men and women rated all items on the questionnaire high, low, and in-between. However, as a whole, women rated extraverted Feeling more highly than men did, even women who rated Thinking items higher than Feeling items over-all. Similarly, as a whole, men rated introverted Thinking items more highly than women did, even men who rated Feeling items higher than Thinking items overall. This difference was statistically significant. A weaker pattern (nonsignificant) was observed for introverted Feeling for women and extraverted Thinking for men.

Gender Links to Lifelong Development

A relationship was observed between gender, age, and how many and which processes are used. Men in their thirties and forties reported extensive advanced use of their preferred processes, with minimal use of nonpreferred processes. Women in their thirties and forties reported

extensive basic use of all processes but less advanced use of their preferred processes. This result fits with research on gender and cognition that suggests women have more interconnectivity between various
areas of the brain, while men tend to have more compartmentalization
between areas and more focused specialization. Our results appear to
contradict hypotheses that interconnectivity is characteristic of Feeling
and compartmentalization is characteristic of Thinking since the pattern held true even for women who preferred Thinking and men who
preferred Feeling.

Many of these results match those of an earlier rigorous research study.
Steve Myers conducted a very large study on how people spend energy to
use the cognitive processes while engaged in teamwork.[11] Among other
results, he observed that processes have basic and advanced aspects, that
processes paralleling our own tend to be least preferred, and that preferred cognitive processes tend to match a person's four-letter type code.
Steve Myers's study is an appropriate comparison since older studies,
such as those done by Singer-Loomis[12] and Grey-Wheelwright,[13] tend to
use significantly different definitions of the cognitive processes and did
not consider critical distinctions, such as passive use versus active use.
We look forward to more discussion and research into Jung's timeless
conception of the psyche.

Notes

1. With credit to Linda V. Berens and John Beebe. For more information on tandem use, see the bibliography. Linda V. Berens contributed some examples of tandem use found in later chapters.

2. Roger Pearman, "Type Consilience Unifying Knowledge on Type Development: Propositions, Questions, and Cogitations," http://www.qualifying.org/about/typeConsilience.pdf (2004).

3. We owe much gratitude to Dr. Sue A. Cooper for identifying the BLM syndrome and thank her for letting us use this valuable acronym in so many places. S. Cooper, "How to Stop Behaving Like Yourself and Start Listening" (presented at APT-X, the Tenth Biennial International Conference of the Association for Psychological Type, July 1993), cassette recording no. F196-117AB. (Garden Grove, CA: InfoMedix).

4. This table is adapted from Linda V. Berens, "The Communication Zone®," in *Dynamics of Personality Type: Understanding and Applying Jung's Cognitive Processes* (Huntington Beach, CA: Telos Publications, 2000), 49.

5. We thank Vicky Jo Varner for suggesting this metaphor.

6. Carl Jung, *Psychological Types* (repr., Princeton, NJ: Princeton University Press, 1971).

7. ibid., 406, paragraph 669.

8. ibid., 402, paragraph 663.

9. ibid., 366, paragraph 611 and 658.

10. ibid., 400, paragraph 658.

11. S. P. Myers, (2001, June). "Research into the Nature and Usage of the Function-Attitudes: Theory and Research Symposium—Dynamic Type and Type Dynamics," in *Symposia Proceedings of APT-XIV, the Fourteenth Biennial International Conference of the Association for Psychological Type* (Minneapolis: Association of Psychological Type, 2001), 81–87

12. M. E. Loomis, "A New Perspective for Jung's Typology: The Singer-Loomis Inventory of Personality," *Journal of Analytical Psychology*, 27, no 1. (1982): 59-69.

13. M. A. Mattoon and M. Davis, "The Gray-Wheelwright Jungian Type Survey: Development and History," *Journal of Analytical Psychology*, 40, no. 2 (1995): 205–234.

Bibliography

Beebe, John. "Understanding Consciousness through the Theory of Psychological Types." In *Analytical Psychology: Contemporary Perspectives in Jungian Analysis*, edited by Joseph Cambray and Linda Carter, 83–115. Hove, England, and New York: Brunner-Routledge, 2004.

Berens, Linda. *Dynamics of Personality Type: Understanding and Applying Jung's Cognitive Processes*. Huntington Beach, CA: Telos Publications, 1999.

Berens, Linda. "The Tandem Principle, Part 1." *Bulletin of Psychological Type* 26, no. 4 (2003).

Berens, Linda. "The Tandem Principle, Part 2." *Bulletin of Psychological Type* 27, no. 1 (2004).

Berens, Linda, and Dario Nardi. *Understanding Yourself and Others®: An Introduction to the Personality Type Code*. Huntington Beach, CA: Telos Publications, 2004.

Grant, Harold, Magdala Thompson, and Thomas Clark. *From Image to Likeness*. Ramsey, NJ: Paulist Press, 1983.

Harris, Anne Singer. *Living with Paradox*. Pacific Grove, CA: Brooks/Cole Publishing Company, 1996.

Hartzler, Gary, and Margaret Hartzler. *Functions of Type: Activities for Developing the Eight Jungian Functions*. Huntington Beach, CA: Telos Publications, 2004.

Jung, Carl. *Psychological Types*. Reprint, Princeton, NJ: Princeton University Press, 1960.

Kegan, Robert. *The Evolving Self*. Boston, Mass: Harvard University Press, 1983.

Lowen, Walter. *Dichotomies of the Mind: A Systems Science Model of Mind and Personality*. New York: John Wiley and Sons, 1982.

Myers, Isabel Briggs. *Gifts Differing.* With Peter B. Myers. 1980. Reprint, Palo Alto, CA: Consulting Psychologists Press, 1995.

Myers, Katherine, and Linda Kirby. *Introduction to Type® Dynamics and Development.* Palo Alto, CA: Consulting Psychologists Press, 1994.

Myers, Steve. "Working Out Your Team Role," (2000), http://www .teamtechnology.co.uk/workingoutyourteamrole.htm

Nardi, Dario. *Multiple Intelligences and Personality Type: Tools and Strategies for Developing Human Potential.* Huntington Beach, CA: Telos Publications, 2001.

Nardi, Dario. "Exploring the Eight Function-Attitudes in Depth." *Bulletin of Psychological Type* 27, no. 1 (2004).

Nardi, Dario. "Roots and Branches: Multiple Models of Type." *Australian Psychological Type Journal* 2, no. 3 (November 2000).

Nardi, Dario. "Type Development Coaching with Neuro-Linguistic Programming." *Bulletin of Psychological Type* 26, no. 2 (2003).

Nardi, Dario. "Type Development: Theory and Research in Context." *Bulletin of Psychological Type* 25, no. 2 (2002).

Nardi, Dario. "Type Dynamics: New Tools for Exploration." *Bulletin of Psychological Type* 25, no. 4 (2002).

O'Connor, and John Seymour. *Introducing NLP: Psychological Skills for Understanding and Influencing People,* 2nd ed. London: Thorsons, 1995.

Pearman, Roger, and Sarah Albritton. *I'm Not Crazy, I'm Just Not You.* Palo Alto, CA: Davies-Black Publishing, 1993.

Pearman, Roger. "Type Consilience—Unifying Knowledge on Type Development: Propositions, Questions, and Cogitations." (2004), http://www.qualifying.org/about/typeConsilience.pdf.

Quenk, Naomi. *In the Grip,* Palo Alto, CA: Consulting Psychologists Press, 1985.

Sharp, Daryl. *Personality Types: Jung's Model of Typology,* Toronto: Inner City Books, 1987.

Thompson, Lenore. *Personality Type: An Owner's Manual.* Boston: Shambhala Publications, 1998.

Dario Nardi, PhD, teaches computer modeling-and-simulation and general honors courses at the University of California, Los Angeles, where he is a founding faculty member of the Human Complex Systems program. Dario has also been a research faculty member with the Temperament Research Institute since 1994 and has been intimately involved in product development and research. He is the author or coauthor of numerous books on personality, including *Multiple Intelligences and Personality Type, Character and Personality Type, Understanding Yourself and Others®: An Introduction to the Personality Type Code,* and *The 16 Personality Types: Descriptions for Self-Discovery.* Dario received his doctorate in systems science from the State University of New York and his bachelor's degree in aerospace engineering from the University of Southern California. His educational background also includes East Asian languages and cultures and creative writing. Dario is the creator of Socialbot™—a virtual, robotic agent capable of socially intelligent behavior, from remembering a person's name in a conversation to conveying its evaluation of one person to another person.

CPSIA information can be obtained
at www.ICGtesting.com
Printed in the USA
FSOW04n1934190116
15720FS